OUTLAW TALES
of California

Other Books by Chris Enss

Pistol Packin' Madams: True Stories of Notorious Women of the Old West

Buffalo Gals: Women of Buffalo Bill's Wild West Show

The Doctor Wore Petticoats: Women Physicians of the Old West

How the West Was Worn: Bustles and Buckskins on the Wild Frontier

Hearts West: True Stories of Mail-Order Brides on the Frontier

Tales Behind the Tombstones: The Deaths and Burials of the Old West's Most Nefarious Outlaws, Notorious Women, and Celebrated Lawmen

The Lady was a Gambler: True Stories of Notorious Women of the Old West

With Howard Kazanjian

The Young Duke: The Early Life of John Wayne

Happy Trails: A Pictorial Celebration of the Life and Times of Roy Rogers and Dale Evans

The Cowboy and the Senorita: A Biography of Roy Rogers and Dale Evans

With Joann Chartier

With Great Hope: Women of the California Gold Rush

Love Untamed: Romances of the Old West

Gilded Girls: Women Entertainers of the Old West

She Wore a Yellow Ribbon: Women Soldiers and Patriots of the Western Frontier

OUTLAW TALES
of California

True Stories of the Golden State's Most Infamous
Crooks, Culprits, and Cutthroats

Chris Enss

TWODOT®

GUILFORD, CONNECTICUT
HELENA, MONTANA
AN IMPRINT OF THE GLOBE PEQUOT PRESS

A · TWODOT® · BOOK

Library of Congress Cataloging-in-Publication Data is available on file.
ISBN 978-0-7627-3852-6

Printed in the United States of America
10 9 8 7 6 5 4 3 2 1

For my brother-in-law, Peter Parry,
an attorney at the Cook County Public Defender's Office,
who faithfully fights for justice

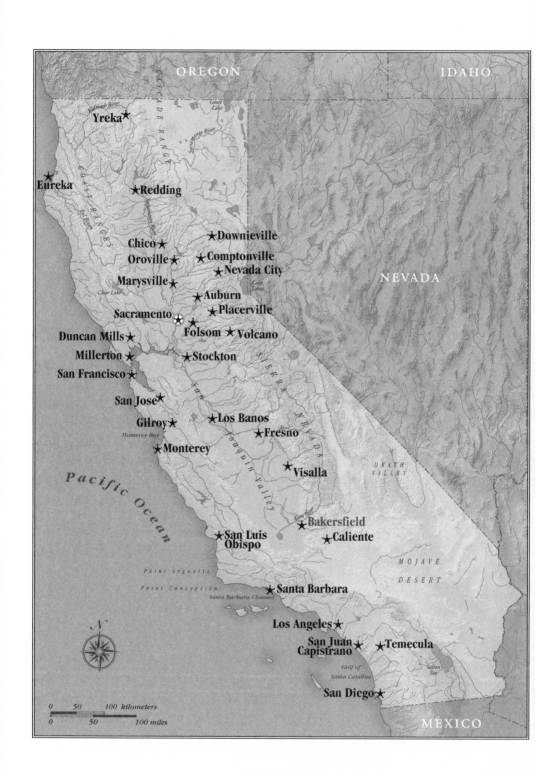

OREGON

IDAHO

Goose
Lake

★ Yreka

Klamath River

NEVADA

Eureka ★

★ Redding

Sacramento River

★ Downieville
Chico ★
Oroville ★   ★ Comptonville
              ★ Nevada City
Marysville ★

Clear Lake

Lake
Tahoe

★ Auburn
Sacramento ★   ★ Placerville
          ☆ ★ Folsom ★ Volcano
Duncan Mills ★

Millerton ★   ★ Stockton
San Francisco ★

SIERRA NEVADA

San Jose ★

Gilroy ★   ★ Los Banos
Monterey Bay   ★ Fresno
★ Monterey

San Joaquin Valley

★ Visalla

DEATH
VALLEY

Kern River

★ Bakersfield
★ San Luis
Obispo   ★ Caliente

MOJAVE

DESERT

Point Arguello

Point Conception

Santa Barbara Channel

★ Santa Barbara

Los Angeles ★

San Juan ★   ★ Temecula
Capistrano

Salton
Sea

Gulf of
Santa Catalina

San Diego ★

Pacific Ocean

COAST RANGES

Eel River

N

0   50   100 kilometers
0   50   100 miles

MEXICO

CALIFORNIA

Contents

Acknowledgments

I am indebted to the following people and organizations for their help in writing this book: Kathy Correia at the California State Library in Sacramento, the San Francisco Museum and Historical Society, the Wells Fargo History Museum, the Santa Cruz Museum and History Library, the San Diego Historical Society, the staff at the Doris Foley Library, and Ed Tyson and the volunteers at Searls Library in Nevada City, California. To all I humbly offer my thanks and appreciation.

Introduction

Stories of the bandits, cattle rustlers, horse thieves, and highwaymen of the Old West have intrigued readers since the first pioneers ventured across the plains. More than 125 years after outlaw Jesse James made a famously candid statement about the public's continuing interest in criminals, people continue to be drawn to the tales of the desperadoes who roamed the wild frontier. As Jesse aptly commented in 1879, "All the world likes an outlaw. For some damn reason they remember them."

A lawless element followed the daring collection of prospectors, hard-working emigrant men and women, and enterprising farmers to the gold fields of California. While civilized pioneers were building churches, schools, theaters, and hotels, thieves and outlaws were terrorizing camp followers, looting mining claims, and robbing Wells Fargo stagecoaches.

Where liquor ran freely, it seemed so did crime. Alcohol often eroded away any effort ambitious sojourners painstakingly made to tame the rowdy territory. Drunkenness, banditry, and violence plagued the California boomtowns, provoking frightened citizens to take the law into their own hands, or appoint willing, but unqualified, peace officers to act on their behalf.

Many of the outlaws who dominated sections of the rugged territory were desperate men who were once honest members of the community, but who felt forced by circumstances into a life of evil. In the later part of the 1860s, a majority of the offenders were veterans of the Civil War, ex-Confederate soldiers like Cole Younger, Frank Dalton, and Ben Thompson, who were convinced they no longer had a country of their own, or a choice but to become a criminal.

Outlaw Tales of California contains the tales and adventures of the most famous rebels and brigands in California's history. Listed among the wanted men of long ago are Black Bart, the notorious highwayman who rarely left the scene of a crime without leaving a poem behind; John Allen, the barber turned horse thief also known as Sheet-Iron Jack; and the most feared bandit of all, "Bloody" Joaquin Murieta.

Although gold initially attracted unscrupulous characters to the northern section of the state, the crimes committed by outlaws chronicled in this book were not limited to that area. Hardened wrongdoers like Jesús Tejada and Juan Flores performed their nefarious activities primarily in Southern California.

By 1850 much of the state, and San Francisco specifically, was so overrun by murderers, horse thieves, and highwaymen that hundreds of law-abiding citizens banded together to enact swift justice against all desperadoes. There were no jails as of yet, and no official court system had been established. Impromptu hearings to try offenders were held and they were either driven out of the city or hanged if they were found guilty of a crime that merited—or even suggested—it.

The February 18, 1858, edition of the *San Francisco Call* gave an example of the quick action law breakers could expect at the hand of determined vigilante committees.

"A man named Aaron Bracey," the article read, "who owned a little place in the northern part of Auburn, sold to his neighbor, James Murphy, a piece of his land. They met near their boundary line, and in an altercation Bracey struck Murphy on the head with a pick-axe, opening his head and exposing the brain. Bracey gave himself up to the officers, and citizens cared for Murphy, who, before he died, explained how he received his wound. Bracey was lodged in jail; but in the evening it was rumored that he would be liberated and lynched.

"About 2:30 o'clock next morning, some sixty-five men overpowered the Sheriff and deputies and took the jail keys, though in their impatient haste, the mob burst in the doors with a sledge-hammer, and Bracey was taken to the edge of town and hanged. Father Quinn, of Sacramento, who had come up to see Murphy, interceded for the prisoner and tried to quiet the mob, but without avail."

The serious, no-nonsense reputation of numerous vigilante committees spread quickly throughout the outlaw community. The fear of retribution at the hands of these committees caused some desperadoes to abandon their illegal ways, but others fiercely defied the unofficial constabularies. Juan Soto, John Sontag, and Chris Evans taunted vigilante teams by perpetrating even more crimes in broad daylight. They also openly threatened the lives of anyone who tried to "bring them to heel."

When insolent criminals like Tiburcio Vasquez were eventually apprehended, their executions were public events. Anxious spectators jockeyed for the best position from which to watch the outlaws hang. More than 2,500 people attended Vasquez's hanging in March 1875.

Faced with an abrupt and furious end to their lives, renegades were oftentimes granted the opportunity to write letters to their loved ones. Vasquez wrote to his mother, trying to shed light on the reason for his tragic demise.

"Beloved Mother," he wrote. "Perhaps you are not aware of the difficulties that I have to surmount and overcome every time I feel inclined to open my heart to you by way of a few badly written lines, but I hope you will overlook the little faults and mistakes of your unfortunate son."

Only a few of the most noted criminals, their crimes against California residents, and the punishment they received, have been included in *Outlaw Tales of California*. Their tales serve as a reminder that the Old West was a violent place, and that although the savage misdeeds of some legendary bandits were romanticized, in the end these perpetrators were regarded as nothing more than troubled outlaws.

Tom Bell

Outlaw Doctor

A pair of tired, dust-covered deputies escorted outlaw Tom Bell to a noose dangling off a limb of a sycamore tree. No one spoke a word as the rope was slipped around his thick neck. More than fifty lawmen from Sacramento, Marysville, and Nevada City, California, made up the posse that apprehended Bell at his hideout at Firebaugh's Ferry near the San Joaquin River. The ruthless highwayman and his gang had eluded the law for more than a year. Bell's reign of terror would end here—a mere four hours after he was captured on Monday, October 6, 1856.

Bell held in his hand a pair of letters his executioners allowed him to write before they administered justice. Outside of the firm grip he had on his correspondence, he didn't show the least bit of fear. Judge Joseph Belt, the self-appointed hangman and head of the posse, sauntered over to Bell and looked him in the eye.

"Do you have anything to say for yourself?" he asked. "I have no revelations to make," Bell replied. "I would be grateful, however," he added, "to drink to the health of this party present and hope that no personal prejudice has induced them to execute me." Judge Belt nodded to one of his men, who stepped forward with a bottle of whisky and offered it to Bell.

Bell lifted the bottle to the men and thanked them for their thoughtfulness. "I have no bitterness toward anyone of you," he said. He took a drink and handed the bottle back to the lawman. "If you let me now . . . before I go. I'd like to read aloud the letter I wrote to my mother." Judge Belt scanned the faces of his men; no one seemed to have any objections.

1

"Go on," Belt told the bandit. Tom unfolded one of the letters in his hand and began reading.

"Dear Mother, I am about to make my exit to another country. I take this opportunity to write you a few lines. Probably you may never hear from me again. If not, I hope we may meet where parting is no prodigal career in this country. I have always recollected your fond admonitions, and if I had lived up to them I would not have been in my present position; but, dear mother, though my fate has been a cruel one, yet I have no one to blame but myself.

"Give my respects to all my old and youthful friends. Tell them to beware of bad associations, and never to enter into any gambling saloons, for that has been my ruin. If my old grandmother is living, remember me to her. With these remarks, I bid you farewell forever. Your only boy, Tom."

Bell refolded his letter and bowed his head in prayer. Two lawmen stepped forward, took the letters from him, and tied his hands behind his back. Tom lifted his head and nodded to Judge Belt. His horse was whipped out from under him and he swung into space.

Tom Bell's real name was Thomas J. Hodges. He was born in Alabama in 1826 and raised in Rome, Tennessee. His parents were upstanding citizens in the community and made sure their son received the finest education. The early talent he had for healing prompted him to become a doctor. Not long after graduating from medical school, he joined the U.S. Army and fought in the Mexican-American War. He served honorably as a noncommissioned officer and was an expert with a rifle and bayonet.

Bell stood over six feet tall, had blue eyes, sandy hair, and a blond mustache and goatee. His most distinguished physical characteristic was his nose. The once shapely and classic feature had been broken at the bridge and lay flat against his face.

Apart from his unforgettable appearance, he had personal magnetism and natural leadership qualities. People from all walks of life were

Dr. Thomas J. Hodges, aka Tom Bell, terrorized the countryside around the mining town of Nevada City, California, in the mid-1850s. *Courtesy of Searls Historical Library.*

drawn to him: teachers and soldiers believed he would be a success in any field of endeavor.

Swept away by the gold crazy exuberance of the day, Tom Bell chose to abandon any thought of a medical career or the military in favor of going west. He hoped to strike it rich in California. He arrived in Nevada County in 1856 and began his life as a prospector on the American River. He soon realized that finding a fortune in gold wasn't as easy a job as the articles in the newspapers back East had led him to imagine. Eventually he traded the hard life of mining for work as a gambler in saloons and dance halls.

Bell had no talent for cards and lost what little money he brought with him to the Gold Country. Destitute and desperate he decided to embark on a life of crime and stole gold dust from a miner's cabin. Caught in the act, Bell was arrested, convicted of grand larceny, and sentenced to five years in jail. When authorities booked him into the state prison on Angel Island, he did not give them his real name. He used the handle of a little-known cattle thief, Tom Bell.

The educated outlaw was in jail for nine months before he found a way that his background in medicine could be used to his advantage. The facility did not have a doctor on the premises, and after learning that seriously ill inmates were sent off the island for treatment, Bell decided to fake an ailment. His experience and knowledge of the workings of the human body helped to make the act convincing. The warden at Angel Island sent Tom to the county jail in San Francisco for treatment. The novice physician there diagnosed Bell's symptoms as serious and prescribed a regimen of exercises and extended liberties for him. It was precisely what the highwayman had hoped for and he used the opportunity to escape.

Bell wasn't alone when he broke out of jail; outlaws Bill Gristy, Ned Connor, and Jim Smith accompanied the doctor. The four escaped convicts formed the nucleus of what would be one of the most notorious gangs in California. Within a month Tom Bell's band of outlaws consisted of more than fifty men. The choice spirits who rode with Bell yielded to his superior intellect and ability and kept state officials in a fever of excitement for nearly two years.

The desperadoes rendezvoused at a hideout in the foothills near Auburn. Bell methodically planned their crimes from there and dispatched groups of men to carry out various holdups. During the spring and summer of 1856, scarcely a night passed when some lonely traveler, the owner of a mercantile or a saloon or a cattle rancher, wasn't forced to stare into the muzzle of a persuading revolver while he was being relieved of his money or livestock.

Foothill residents and business owners, tired of being victimized, wanted Bell and his men stopped. But local peace officers were unable to apprehend the clever thieves. Newspapers ran scathing editorials about the inadequacies of law enforcement and challenged the government to organize a ranger company to bring in Bell.

"What is the result of this failure to catch one who is, after all, only an ordinary man? It is incumbent upon our state authorities to take immediate steps in the premises," suggested the *Sacramento Union*.

But California governor J. Neely Johnson refused to intercede stating that a "special act of legislature was necessary before a state mandated posse could be assembled."

With no one capable of stopping them, Tom Bell and his gang continued to terrorize highway travelers, holding up numerous miners and peddlers and robbing countless pack trains and wagons. Unlike some of the other outlaws of the time who treated their victims cruelly, physically abusing them or shooting them on the spot, Bell had a reputation as a bandit who avoided bloodshed if at all possible. He was considerate of his prey and never left them completely destitute. Bell and his men held up a wagon near Volcano, California, and demanded that the driver turn over his money. The stunned man handed Bell all he had, which amounted to $30.25. Bell took the cash, but returned the coin to the driver and told him to "buy a drink and forget the incident."

In another wagon robbery, Bell and his men stole $3,000 in gold dust. Before riding away they blindfolded the driver and tied him to a tree. The man's hands were purposely tied in a loose fashion, however. Not long after Bell's gang had fled the scene, the driver broke free, and when he removed his blindfold, he saw that Bell had left him food and a hunting knife.

On occasion the outlaw doctor utilized his surgical skills to assist targets injured in the process of being robbed. A gambler traveling from Downieville to Marysville resisted being held up by Bell and his men. He fired on the gang and was brought down by a bullet in the thigh. Before dressing the wound, Bell relieved the man of his money. He placed the gambler in the back of a wagon that had innocently happened onto the scene. After instructing the driver to turn over any money he had on him, he told the man to take care of the bleeding victim he would now be transporting. "Drive slowly and pick your road," Bell warned him.

Tom Bell's gang had a knack for stealing from the wealthiest travelers on the road. The secret of their talent was the cooperation of the proprietors of the Mountaineer House Stage Stop, the California House Hotel and Saloon, and the Western Exchange Hotel (brothels and eateries in the Gold Country). Each owner was paid a handsome sum to supply Bell with information about rich customers. Bell's men would hang around inside the establishments and wait for the owners to point out the person they were to rob. One such traveler was Solomon D. Barstow, a Wells Fargo security agent guarding mule trains for a mining company.

On March 12, 1856, Barstow, the driver, and three of his men were transporting $21,000 in gold dust to a bank in the Bay Area. Tom Bell's gang got the jump on them at the base of the Trinity Mountains. Bell and his men were armed with double-barreled shotguns. They wore red flannel shirts, black silk handkerchiefs with eyeholes cut out, and red skullcaps. Barstow attempted to go for his gun, but Bell advised him against it. "Stop it!" Bell barked. "We don't want to kill you, but we will." Barstow and his men complied. Tom Bell's gang tied the driver and his help to trees and robbed them of their own money as well as taking off with the gold shipment. The heist was the biggest armed robbery of the Gold Rush and Tom Bell was now the most wanted man in the West.

The police searched several counties in northern California looking for Bell, but they had no luck. The seeming ease with which Bell was able to elude the law made him more confident in his abilities. Convinced he was invincible, he began making plans to rob a stage. Robbing a stage was a relatively new idea. Up to this point, it had only been done once, in 1853. Bell was positive he could do the job.

The bandits decided to hold up a coach traveling from Camptonville to Marysville. Bell and his men hid out at the California House and planned the robbery. Bell sent one of the gang members out to nose around Camptonville and find out when any large gold shipments would be leaving town. After a few days the gang member returned with news of $100,000 in gold dust being sent on the down stage, the stage "down" to Marysville. Bell acted fast, planting one of his men inside the stage disguised as a miner and setting up an ambush at a fork in the road where the vehicle was to pass.

Much of the gold dust on the stage belonged to a businessman known only to history as Mr. Rideout. Rideout rode ahead of the stage on horseback. He led the coach down the wilderness road and was soon surrounded by Tom and two of his men. Bell knocked the startled Rideout off his horse, leaving him unconscious and afoot, then hurried off to meet the rest of his men. The other members of Bell's gang were a few miles back, overtaking the stage. They ordered the driver to stop, but the driver only whipped the team on faster. Infuriated, Bell's men opened fire.

Several passengers on the stage drew their weapons and forty or so shots were rapidly exchanged at close quarters. The outlaws were not prepared for such a fierce resistance and they pulled back . . . but not before killing one female passenger and injuring two male passengers. When the coach arrived in Marysville, the driver reported the attempted holdup and a posse was quickly formed. Rideout, having regained consciousness and found his horse, arrived in town just as the posse was heading out.

The posse, led by William King, captain of the Marysville police, was just one of a half dozen organized to apprehend Bell. Detectives with a Sacramento posse were instructed by their sheriff to "capture or destroy Tom Bell and his band."

In the whole history of California's early days, there was never a more united effort to run a criminal down. After a short time combing the countryside for Bell and his gang, the posses returned empty-handed. Nothing gave Bell more confidence than thwarting the law's attempts to bring him in. In a letter to Captain King, Bell taunted his officers and dared them to come after him.

"My dear Captain King . . . don't think for a moment that your vigilance causes me any uneasiness, or that I seek for an armistice. No, far from it, for I have unfurled my banner to the breeze, and my motto is, 'Catch me if you can!'"

King and the other posse leaders accepted Bell's challenge and beefed up their efforts to capture the outlaw and his men. Rewards were posted and citizens who recognized members of Bell's gang came forward. One by one the posse brought in Bell's men, each informing on another. Bill Gristy, Bell's right-hand man, was captured by Judge Joseph Belt and his posse and he led them to the gang's main hideout. The spot was a large ranch laid out in a hidden valley along the San Joaquin River.

Judge Belt and his deputies snuck up on Bell as he was riding toward his ranch house. They leveled their guns at him and he raised his hands slowly over his head. "I believe that you are the man we have been looking for," Belt said. "Very probably," Tom coolly replied. Judge Belt ordered his men to tie Bell up and the bandit did not resist.

The notion that Tom Bell was entitled to due process of the law did not sit well with Judge Belt. The judge felt Tom should be given the same mercy he had shown the men and women he robbed, injured, or killed. Belt and the others decided to hang him vigilante style.

Judge Belt took possession of the letters Bell wrote, which were later printed in the *San Francisco Alta* newspaper. Readers reacted appropriately to the letter Bell wrote to his mother, but his second correspondence prompted a great deal of controversy. It outlined his wishes for his young mistress. The letter was written to Mrs. Elizabeth Hood, owner of the Western Exchange Hotel. Hood harbored the outlaw on a number of occasions and he had developed affection for her three daughters, ages nine, eleven, and fourteen. It is rumored he was romantically involved with the oldest girl, Sarah, but Mrs. Hood emphatically denied they had that kind of relationship.

In any event, Bell cared enough for her children to use the last few hours of his life to pen a letter bidding them farewell.

"Mrs. Hood, my dear and only friend now in this country: As I am not allowed the liberty of seeing you, I have been given the privilege of writing you a few lines, as I have but a few moment[s] to live. I am at a great loss for something to say. I have been most fully betrayed. Bill has told things that never took place. I am accused of every robbery that has been committed for the past twelve months, which is entirely false. I have never committed but three highway robberies in my life; but still I am to blame and my fate is sealed. I am to die like a dog, and there is but one thing that grieves me, and that is the condition of you and your family. Probably I have been the instrumentality of your misfortunes.

"I would like to give you some advice but I fear you may think me presumptuous. What I would say is this: That you had better send the girls to San Francisco to the Sisters of Charity. There they will be educated and taken care of. Tell all the girls farewell! Tell them to be good girls and to be very careful to whom they pledge themselves for life.

"All the money I have is ten dollars, which I have given to Mr. Chism for Sarah. I must come to a close, for the hounds are thirsting for my blood. Good-bye forever."

Thirty-one-year-old Tom Bell's career as the Gold Country's most dangerous, but gentlemanly, outlaw had lasted only eighteen months.

Tiburcio Vasquez
A Spirit of Revenge

A light, frigid rain tapped the dirty windows of a small store located along the banks of the San Joaquin River near the town of Millerton, California. A half-dozen ferryboat operators were inside soaking up the warmth emanating from a fireplace. Four of them were huddled around a table playing cards, the other two were enjoying a drink at a makeshift bar, while an unkempt clerk arranged a row of canned goods across a warped shelf.

The clerk was entertaining the preoccupied men in the room with a song when the shop door swung open. He was the last to notice the figures standing in the entrance way. He looked up from his work after becoming conscious of his own loud voice in the sudden silence. He slowly turned to see what everyone else was staring at.

The outlaw Tiburcio Vasquez entered the store with his pistol drawn. Three other desperadoes, all brandishing weapons, followed closely behind. Vasquez, a handsome man of medium height with large, light-grey eyes, surveyed the terrified faces of the patrons as he smoothed down his brown mustache and goatee. "Put up your hands," he ordered the men. The clerk quickly complied and the others reluctantly did the same.

Two more of Vasquez's men burst into the store through the back entrance and leveled their guns on the strangers before them. "You don't need a gun here," the clerk tried to reason with the bandits. Vasquez grinned as he walked over to the man. "Yes, I do," he said as he placed his gun against the clerk's temple. "It helps quiet my nerves." Vasquez demanded that the men drop to the floor, facedown. After they had complied, their hands and feet were tied behind them. One of the men

11

The ruthless Tiburcio Vasquez was hanged in 1875 for his many crimes.
Courtesy of Searls Historical Library.

cursed the desperadoes as he struggled to free himself. "You damned bastard," he shouted at Vasquez. "If I had my six-shooter, I'd show you whether I'd lie down or not."

The bandits laughed at the outburst and proceeded to rob the store and its occupants of $2,300. The November 10, 1873, holdup was one of more than one hundred such raids perpetrated by the thirty-eight-year-old Mexican and his band of cutthroat thieves and murderers in their violent careers. The desperadoes escaped the scene of the crime, eluding authorities for a full year before they were caught.

Prior to the Gold Rush, California's population was composed primarily of the original Spanish and Mexican settlers and indigenous Native Americans. News of the riches found in the foothills of the territory loosed a flood of white settlers into the area. In the pioneers' quest to tame the Wild West and transform the fertile California frontier into a "civilized" state, native Californians were forced into a new way of life. Families like Tiburcio Vasquez's harbored a great deal of animosity toward the white miners and businessmen who demanded that the original residents conform to their laws and way of living. Vasquez resented such treatment and from an early age began rebelling against what he called the "gringo's" influence.

Born in Monterey County, California, on August 11, 1837, Tiburcio was one of six children. His mother, Maria, was the daughter of explorer José Guadalupe Contua. His father, José, was a farmer who struggled to provide for his wife and family. Homesteaders from the East encroached on his land, making it difficult for him to compete for a share of the agricultural market. When Tiburcio was old enough to contribute financially, he took the only job he believed he could find, that of a cattle rustler and horse thief. He justified his outlawry by blaming the "Americans" for his lack of employment opportunity.

At the age of seventeen, Vasquez went into business with a friend, using his ill-gotten gains to become the co-owner of a dance hall. The fandango proved to be profitable, but was not without its share of problems. The white settlers who frequented the place treated the Mexican women who worked there badly, calling them names and insulting their ethnicity. Their actions further fueled the hatred Vasquez had for them.

Many wealthy Mexicans did not share Vasquez's opinion of the Americans. They disapproved of his criminal activities and refused to associate with him. One particular rancher, aware that his only daughter was romantically involved with the teenage bandit, forbade him from seeing her. When Vasquez disobeyed the order and kidnapped the man's daughter, the outraged rancher pursued the pair. The defiant young man refused to give up the girl, her father pulled a gun on him, and a gunfight broke out. Vasquez turned his paramour over only after he was shot in the arm.

Shortly after Vasquez's arm had mended he was involved in another confrontation, this time with a constable. The dispute resulted in the death of the lawman.

At eighteen Vasquez was a fugitive on the run and he would remain so for two years. The ambitious criminal's natural leadership qualities attracted many like-minded desperadoes who joined forces with him. Together they robbed numerous stores and lone travelers in northern California.

The authorities apprehended the outlaw in 1857. He was tried for his crimes and sentenced to five years in San Quentin. Vasquez escaped after ten months behind bars and was recaptured in 1859. After serving his time he was released, but within six months was charged with another robbery and sent back to jail. On August 3, 1870, he left prison again. He was a free, but not reformed, man.

Vasquez gathered together another group of bandits and started robbing stagecoaches traveling between San Francisco and Los Angeles, in rapid succession. He and his fellow desperadoes murdered numerous men during their holdups and gunned down any posse that tried to stop them.

One of the most heinous crimes committed by Vasquez and his men occurred in August 1873. The band of outlaws overtook a shop owner in the village of Tres Pinos in Monterey County and stole money from his register and the safe. Then they proceeded to make their way through the town, looting and vandalizing businesses.

Vasquez shot three innocent men. One of the members of his gang struck down a young boy, rendering him unconscious. After taking everything of value, the bandits rode off into the night. The terrorized community was outraged by Vasquez's savagery, a posse was formed, and an $8,000 reward was offered for his capture.

Undeterred by the swarm of lawmen on their trail, Vasquez and his cohorts continued their crime spree, holding up a number of stores and stages in the San Joaquin Valley. Among the most ruthless of those robberies occurred in the town of Kingston. Vasquez attacked the hamlet in the dead of night and ordered his gang to tie up all the male citizens. One by one he stripped them of their personal possessions and money and then cleaned out the stores and hotel.

California citizens were furious over the outlaw's violent raids and at the inability of law enforcement officers to stop him. Gov. Newton Booth responded to his constituents' cry for justice and appointed the tough, respected Alameda County sheriff Harry Morse to recruit a band of deputies to bring down Vasquez. Booth appropriated $5,000 to get the job done.

When word reached Vasquez that a highly trained posse had been formed, he decided the outlaws should disband for a while. Vasquez retreated to the Valley of the Cahuengas near Los Angeles and hid out at a friend's cabin.

Heavy rains in the area hampered Sheriff Morse's hunt for the desperado. His posse spent two months and traveled some 2,700 miles before getting a lead on where Vasquez was staying. In April 1874, the posse received a telegram that told them of a robbery at the San Gabriel Mission, nine miles outside of Los Angeles. Vasquez had been the culprit and, after the attack, he had retreated into the Soledad Mountains.

A woman who lived in the vicinity of the desperado's hideout offered to escort the authorities to him. In exchange for the information the woman, who was rumored to be the expectant mother of Vasquez's child, wanted a portion of the reward. Sheriff Morse was too far away from the scene to respond in a timely fashion and a San Diego sheriff was asked to attend to the matter. The sheriff heard what the woman had to say, but he felt she was lying about what she knew and refused to investigate the tip.

The search for Vasquez continued for another month. Morse combed the terrain in the north and Los Angeles sheriff William Rowland covered the southern portion of the state.

On May 13, 1874, Sheriff Rowland and his posse, which included George A. Beers, a sharp-shooting reporter from the *San Francisco Chronicle*, tracked the criminal down. Vasquez was exactly where the informant had told authorities he was four weeks before. When the bandit was alerted that the posse was closing in he tried to make a run for it. Beers took aim with his shotgun and sent a volley of pellets into the bandit. Vasquez survived his injuries and was transported to Los Angeles to stand trial.

The news that the savage gunmen had been taken into custody spread quickly across the state. Curious citizens congregated at the jail to get a look at the notorious outlaw. An article in the *Los Angeles Star* on May 16, 1874, described the commotion surrounding Vasquez's arrival into the area.

"As the clerk of the City Council was about to read the last communication to that body yesterday, about 4:30 p.m., an unusual stir about the front attracted some attention, and in a moment more, City Fathers, City Clerks, City Surveyors, City Reporters and everybody else in the room, were making for the front door. Instinctively, we supposed Vasquez had something to do with the fuss. We were right. Vasquez was lying pale and bloody in a light wagon, in front of the entrance to the city jail.

"A surging crowd was gathering around. Two men who were taken in his company, at the time of the capture, were taken into the jail and locked up. In a moment after Vasquez himself was lifted from the wagon and was brought into the city prison.

"Dr. Wise presented himself; and assisted by several medical gentlemen of this city, rendered the wounded robber such surgical services he was required . . . The bullets were extracted, the wounds pronounced not dangerous and opinion expressed that he would be well in a few days."

J. M. Bassett, the editor of the *Los Angeles Herald,* was later granted an interview with Vasquez. According to Bassett, although the outlaw was weak and recovering from his wounds, he held a long conversation with him. "His general demeanor is that of a quiet, inoffensive man," Bassett later wrote. "And but for his calm, steady eye, which stamps him as a man of great determination and firmness, no one would take him for the terrible Tiburcio Vasquez."

After Vasquez showed Bassett his leg where the buckshot had been removed, the journalist began asking him questions.

The following is part of the conversation that took place.

"Where are they going to take you now, Vasquez?"

"I don't know," was the reply.

"And I suppose you don't care much now, do you?"

"Oh, well, that is not for me to say. I am not my own master now," (with a shrug of the shoulders).

"Perhaps they will try you on account of your connection with the Tres Pinos affair. How do you think you would get through that?"

"Well, all I know is that I never shot a man in my life. I have had plenty of chances when I have had over five, ten or twenty men tied hand and foot, but I never wanted to shoot anybody."

"Now, Vasquez, you don't really mean to say that you never shot a man in your life?"

"Yes, I do; I never shot a man."

"Do you like your robber life?"

"No, not at all . . . "

"Why did you live such a life, then? Wasn't it your own choice?"

"No, I was obliged to."

"What do you mean by that?"

"I mean that when I tried to settle down anywhere and tried to get a living, they came and drove me out. They wouldn't give me any peace."

"Who are they?"

"Why, the Americans—the officers."

"If you behave yourself they wouldn't meddle with you, would they?"

"Oh yes, they would; that didn't make any difference."

As soon as he was able to travel, the authorities loaded Vasquez aboard a steamer and escorted him to San Francisco. From there he would be moved to San Jose where his trial would be held. Hundreds of people flocked to get a glimpse of the outlaw. They stood outside the jails where he was housed, shouting his name. Some of the crowd was made up of Mexicans who believed Vasquez was a hero; others called him a "miserable, lying murderer," and demanded swift justice.

On January 6, 1875, Tiburcio Vasquez was tried in San Jose for the Tres Pinos murders. The galley was filled with local residents, many of whom visited the criminal in his cell when the hearing concluded each day. In one evening Vasquez received 673 visitors, the majority of them being women who saw the bandit as a folk hero.

Vasquez's trial ended two months after it began. After deliberating for two hours, the jury found him guilty and he was sentenced to hang on March 19, 1875.

As he was being led to the gallows, which had been imported from Sacramento, he offered an explanation for his actions to onlookers. "A spirit of hatred and revenge took possession of me," he said. "I had numerous fights in defense of what I believed to be my rights and those of my countrymen. I believed we were unjustly deprived of the social rights that belonged to us."

Just before he was executed, Vasquez turned to the lawman adjusting the noose around his neck and spoke one last word: "Pronto!" With that the trap door dropped out from under the outlaw and he fell to his death.

John Allen

The Singing Barber

John Allen's mare slowly carried him through a dense grove of trees lining an overgrown trail in Tehama County, California. The sturdy rider sang to himself as he and his horse drifted in and out of the sunlight filtering through a canopy of massive pine and oak trees. If not for the pair of loaded pistols strapped to his waist and the shotgun cradled in his arms, one would have thought he was a traveling musician on his way to entertain prospectors at a mining camp.

Allen was a highwayman and horse thief who sometimes relied on his gifted singing voice to gain the trust of his unsuspecting victims. If his charm and talent as a performer could not separate his victims from the livestock and gold he wanted, he used his ability with a gun to take their possessions.

Born in approximately 1844 in New York, Allen never fit into the mold of the other bandits that roamed the California territory. The five-foot-six, twenty-five-year-old man had the face of an innocent boy, gray eyes, and reddish-brown hair. The unclad ladies and colorful flag tattoos that covered his forearms were as distinctive as was his manner of speech. He was a highly educated individual and spoke with the eloquence of a learned man.

Allen was a barber who decided to seek his fortune beyond the Mississippi. After settling in Shasta County in 1866, he opened a shop to practice his trade. He was personable, witty, and loved to talk. He became increasingly dissatisfied, however, with his modest income and decided to venture into the horse-stealing business.

John Allen robbed several stages carrying passengers and strongboxes in 1876.
Courtesy of California History Section, California State Library.

His customers slowly began to notice that his extravagant lifestyle did not fit the earnings of a simple barber. He spent a great deal of money on prostitutes, alcohol, and celebrating at local saloons. He splurged on the barmaids attracted to his charismatic style and gift for waltzing. Women claimed he "danced like an angel." When he wasn't taking the ladies for a turn on the dance floor, he was playing the guitar and singing. His crisp baritone voice made women swoon.

Although residents in the various mining towns in Shasta County where Allen worked and played suspected the "singing barber" of criminal activities, no one could be sure. It wasn't until a rancher caught Allen stealing three of his best horses that their suspicions were confirmed. Five ranch hands pursued the thief through the local rocky terrain. Allen swore at them as he made his getaway. They fired a volley of shots that ricocheted off the trees and rocks. One of the men let loose a shotgun blast he was sure struck the outlaw. "I heard the bullets strike hard," he told local authorities, "but it didn't stop Allen. It sounded as though I shot at a bird on a tin roof." It was that incident that prompted sheriffs and deputies to begin referring to the desperado as Sheet-Iron Jack.

Undeterred by the possibility of getting caught, Allen roamed the territory stealing more horses from farmers and ranchers and selling them to desperadoes, often time unscrupulous buyers. The more time that passed without his being caught, the more daring Allen became. His criminal activities grew to include robbing lone travelers he came across in the northern valleys. But in May 1871, Sheet-Iron Jack deviated from his outlaw ways to help a lost sojourner he had met while riding through Tehama County.

Digging his heels into the sides of the horse he was riding, Allen emerged from under the trees covering the rocky trail he'd been on and eyed the clearing ahead. Off in the distance he spotted a young man sitting alone on a boulder. He carefully scanned the area to see if there were any other people around, and when it appeared the young man was by himself, Allen trotted his horse over to him.

The man was frightened and a bit disoriented. He had no gear, horse, weapon, or shoes. When he saw Allen, he jumped behind the rock. Allen cautiously dismounted and just as cautiously approached the loner. "What are you doing afoot all the way out here, boy?" the bandit asked. The young man slowly stepped out from his temporary hiding place and flopped down on the ground, tired and embarrassed. Through a thick German accent, he explained to Allen that he was an immigrant on his way to the gold fields. His horse had suffered an injured hoof and he had stopped to contemplate how to proceed when a mountaineer happened along.

The mountaineer inspected the horse's hurt hoof and determined the animal was lame. He told the naïve prospector that it would take a year before the horse was fully healed. He offered to take the animal off the prospector's hands for thirty dollars. The young man decided to accept the offer and trek to the nearest town to get a new horse. He had woefully underestimated the distance to the next stage stop and had been walking so long that his shoes had given out.

As the conversation between the greenhorn and the outlaw continued, Allen learned that he had had his horse shod the day he began his journey. Allen surmised that his horse had gone lame because it had been improperly shod. He'd seen the scam played out on many unsuspecting settlers. A less than honest blacksmith does a poor job on the animal, and his partner in the field then rides out to take the injured horse away for a bargain price.

"You've been swindled," Allen told the lad. "I'm not opposed to it myself, but this is my beat, and nobody has any business doing any swindling here but me!"

Allen turned over a spare pair of boots to the young man and a canteen of water. He instructed him to stay at that spot until he returned. The irritated horse thief hurried off to find the lawbreaker.

Sheet-Iron Jack tracked the opportunistic mountaineer to an isolated canyon and snuck into his camp where his horses were tied to a row of sagebrush. The man had no idea that Allen was anywhere near until he heard him pull the hammer back on his pistol. The mountaineer put his hands up and slowly turned to face the gunman.

"Which one of those ponies belonged to the German boy you robbed?" he demanded. The man motioned to the animal with his head. "I bought that horse, mister," the man snapped back. "That's right," Allen replied. "For thirty dollars. Let's have it," he ordered, taking from the mountaineer the same amount that he'd offered the greenhorn. The frustrated mountaineer reluctantly surrendered his cash.

Allen pocketed the money and with his gun still leveled at the man's head he untied the stolen horse and hopped aboard his own ride. "I'm going to keep that thirty bucks as a lawyer's fee," Allen announced. The man was furious and began cursing and yelling. Allen jumped off his horse and hurried over to the impertinent man and stuck his gun in his stomach. "If you'd kept your mouth shut you'd have been better off," he told him through gritted teeth. "I should have remembered that a lawyer always takes all his client has got."

Allen forced the mountaineer to turn over his weapons and give him all the money he had, which amounted to more than $600. Sheet-Iron Jack rode off warning the swindler to get out of the territory. He escorted the greenhorn's ride back to him and returned it and an additional thirty dollars. After advising the prospector to make sure his horses were properly shoed in the future, Jack sent him on his way.

While making his way to the town of Redding, the German traveler met up with a posse tracking Sheet-Iron Jack. He told them about his encounter with the bandit and that Allen was a good man and his friend and couldn't be the hardened criminal they claimed.

For five years Allen ventured in and out of various northern California counties stealing horses and robbing solitary riders. Thomas Godwin, the sheriff of Tehama County, made it his personal mission to apprehend repeat offenders like Allen. When Sheet-Iron Jack made off with several thoroughbreds within Godwin's jurisdiction, the relentless sheriff vowed to hunt him down and bring him to justice.

Godwin and his deputies had never laid eyes on Allen, but that did not dissuade them from forming a posse to track the horse thief. Armed with sufficient firearms and ammunition, and a description of the outlaw, the sheriff led his men through the countryside to look for Allen.

Like any competent desperado, Allen knew his way around the terrain and was keenly aware of when he was being followed. He spotted the posse from a bluff and decided to investigate. When the group of men bunked down for the night, the bold outlaw sauntered into their camp.

He told the lawmen that he was a concerned landowner who wanted to help stop the criminal element that was roaming the area.

Allen was incredibly personable and a persuasive talker; no one suspected he wasn't being honest. He spent the next day with the posse advising them on the best route to take and speculating on the hideout of the thief. The following evening he led the men to a roadhouse where they decided to stay for the night. Over dinner Allen entertained the men with songs and comical stories. Sheriff Godwin was so impressed with Allen's positive influence over his deputies that he invited him to share his cabin with him.

Before dawn broke Allen slinked out of the inn, taking with him three of the deputies' best horses. When Godwin and the other law enforcement agents awoke and realized Allen had taken off with their rides, they quickly loaded their gear and hurried after him. The posse picked up his trail a few miles south of the roadhouse and followed it to a settler's cabin. The owner of the homestead told the men that Allen had stopped at his place just two hours prior to their arrival. He had watered the horses in his possession and before riding out had asked the man to give the sheriff a letter he had written. The letter thanked Godwin for the company, grub, and the horses.

The posse pursued Sheet-Iron Jack into the wilds of the Trinity Mountains where they lost his trail, never to find it again.

Ranchers in the area would occasionally band together and pick up where the posse left off to try and locate Allen and the livestock he stole from them. Because he rode alone he was able to lose himself in narrow canyon passage and dense brush where large groups of men could not follow. Even with this advantage, the brazen bandit could not resist tempting fate. It was not unusual for him to linger a bit at any of the towns he was passing through while on the run. On one instance he attended a Saturday night social and danced with a half-dozen women before hurrying off into the night.

In mid-1876, Allen's luck finally ran out. He stopped at a saloon in Shasta and ordered too much to drink. The inebriated renegade started a fight with another patron and shot him during the altercation. Allen was arrested and thrown in jail. His trial was quick, but his charm prevailed. The judge sentenced the likeable outlaw to two years in prison.

Within a week after the hearing, Allen was transported to San Quentin. The stage he was riding in was held up just outside of town.

The two robbers escaped after exchanging several bullets with the deputies onboard the coach. Appalled by their actions, the handcuffed Allen stuck his upper body out of the window of the stage and began shouting at the criminals. The figure of the restrained passenger caught their attention; they reconsidered their actions and retreated.

An article about the incident appeared in the next day's edition of the *Shasta Courier*. The editor wrote that "Sheet-Iron Jack cussed the robbers until the very air smelled of brimstone, and small streaks of lightening flashed from his mouth and played in fiery circles around his head. He said that it was an unmitigated outrage that a man could not be permitted to travel over Shasta County territory, especially when he was on his way to work for the interest of the state, without having his life endangered by shots fired by murderous highwaymen."

The robbery attempt did not stop authorities from taking Allen on to San Quentin. His stay at the prison was short lived, however, because a gifted attorney found a problem in the sentencing. The technicality made it possible for Allen to be released after only five months of incarceration. The thief was retried, errors were corrected, and he was sentenced for a second time.

Allen escaped a week after his second appearance at San Quentin. The failed stagecoach robbery he had witnessed prompted the outlaw to attempt his own stage holdup. Instead of taking on such a job alone, Allen recruited the help of two other escaped convicts. From November 6 to November 11, 1876, the three men robbed five stages. Allen's cohorts did not lie low after the crime the way he did. They were careless and quickly caught drinking the night away at a saloon in Shasta County.

The unscrupulous outlaws confessed their crime to the sheriff and led the lawmen and his deputies to the place where Allen was hiding out. Sheet-Iron Jack was captured and the three men were tried and convicted. By December 1876, Allen was on his way back to San Quentin to spend the next twenty-four years of his life at the facility.

In 1882, California governor George Perkins was prevailed on by Allen to review his case. The good argument he made for such a request, combined with his exceptional behavior behind bars, encouraged the governor to consider the matter. Perkins looked over the case against Allen and concluded that he had been convicted on insufficient evidence. On June 25, 1883, his sentence was commuted, but he was ordered to leave California and never return.

Sheet-Iron Jack did not leave the state. He returned to his old haunts and way of living. He was arrested again in the summer of 1884 for stealing horses and robbing a stage stop. He served his lengthy term in Folsom Prison and when he was released in 1895 he moved to Oregon and lived out the rest of his days on a Modoc Indian reservation.

Juan Soto

Human Wildcat

Sheriff Harry Morse removed a Sharp & Hankins carbine rifle from the leather holster on his saddle and opened its sliding barrel. He surveyed the sprawling canyon deep in the heart of the Panoche Mountains, fifty miles outside of Gilroy, California. In the distance below were three small adobe houses, and Morse had every reason to believe that Juan Soto, the thief and murderer he'd been tracking, was held up inside one of the buildings.

High above the sheriff and his seven-member posse was a seemingly inexhaustible mat of black, rainless clouds moving steadily across the world. Morse watched the sun disappear behind the billows and nodded to the deputies on horseback on either side of him. Two groups of three riders began their descent into the valley. Sheriff Morse and the lawmen next to him followed closely behind.

Juan Soto, the outlaw who had been the driving force behind the posse's five-week search, had a reputation for brutality. For more than four years, the six-foot-two, 220-pound half-Indian, half-Mexican man had terrorized the area from the Livermore Valley to San Luis Obispo. Soto and his gang of desperadoes robbed stages, stage stops, lone emigrants, and prospectors. Their victims were oftentimes beaten or killed. Soto's dark features and general expression of animal ferocity earned him the name "the human wildcat." He had black, slightly crossed eyes; a narrow forehead; a mane of black hair; and a busy beard and mustache. The April 10, 1871, edition of the *San Francisco Chronicle* described his appearance as the "physical manifestation of as cruel a spirit as ever animated a human being."

Outlaw Juan Soto was known as "The Human Wildcat." *Courtesy California History Section, California State Library.*

Convinced that law enforcement would be too afraid of him and his men to ultimately capture him, Soto rested comfortably at his hideout. Surrounded by gang members and their paramours, he planned their next job in between hands of poker. Like the famous outlaw who mentored him, Tiburcio Vasquez, Soto believed the crimes he perpetrated on white settlers were justified. American pioneers were viewed by many California natives as people who would remove any obstacle to take over and settle the land.

Soto hated the Americans who were slowly establishing law and order in the territory. On January 10, 1871, Soto and his gang planned and executed a crime they believed would demonstrate the depth of their resentment toward the determined settlers they referred to as "piggish gringos."

A Sunol store clerk, known throughout the tiny village in Alameda County as Otto Ludovici, tidied the shelves and swept the floor of the business after a long day's work. The store owner's wife, Mrs. Thomas Scott, and her three children were assisting in the routine of closing the business by refilling candy jars, folding bolts of fabric, and restacking blankets. Otto weaved past his helpers, walked over to the door and locked it. As he turned the key a large rock shattered the front window. The door suddenly flew open and Juan Soto and several of his rough associates stepped inside.

Mrs. Scott gathered her terrified children close to her. Otto slowly backed away from the bandits unsure of what to do next. "I'm afraid we're closed now," the petrified clerk stammered. "We'll open again in the morning." Soto laughed a little at how frightened the man appeared. "I don't plan to buy anything, señor . . . today or tomorrow," the desperado said coldly. "But take . . . that I will do."

Otto cast a glance at a rifle on the counter next to him, but before he could make a move Soto pulled out his six-gun and shot the clerk in the chest. The man fell to the floor in a heap.

Mrs. Scott hurried her children out of the room and down the hall and quickly disappeared with them into a storage area. A sly smile of content spread across Soto's face as he watched them flee. While his outlaw group looted the store, Soto cocked his gun and fired several volleys in the direction of the place where Mrs. Scott and her brood were hiding. Their screams filled the air and they could be heard crying. Soto then reloaded his weapon and assisted the bandits in looting the store.

The crooks were so preoccupied with the robbery they did not notice Mrs. Scott run out the back door with her youngsters in tow. Soto looked up just in time to see them scurry across the street into a neighbor's house. Before he and his men fled the shop unopposed, Soto kicked the dead clerk in the side and cursed the deceased for his "unfortunate circumstance."

The desperado's barbaric and depraved behavior incensed the residents in town and sent waves of terror washing over the outlying areas.

Law-abiding citizens may have been terrified of Soto, calling him "the most fearsome figure of an outlaw that ever roamed," but Harry Morse, Alameda County's tough, no-nonsense sheriff, vowed to go to the ends of the earth to "track Soto down and see that his head was placed in a noose." Morse was known as a persistent manhunter and had brought several noted California criminals like Norrato Ponee and Tiburcio Vasquez to justice. He was no less determined to capture Soto.

In February 1871, Sheriff Morse and his posse were combing the rough terrain in central California in search of Soto and his gang. After three days of traveling over jumbled rocks and narrow pathways, Morse and his deputies had not seen any signs of human life. They were about to alter the direction of their search when they caught sight of a lone sheepherder. It took considerable persuasion, but the man finally agreed to lead the sheriff to the place where Soto and the other bandits were camped.

Once Morse's posse had surrounded the houses where Soto and his gang were hiding out, the sheriff and another lawman walked their horses into the camp. Posing as a pair of lost riders, the sheriff approached the corral and exchanged pleasantries with an unsuspecting stable worker. Morse told the man he was thirsty and asked him for a drink.

The man nodded approvingly. The lawmen dismounted and he led them to the main house. The sheriff was carrying a revolver with him and his partner was holding a double-barreled shotgun loaded with buckshot. The naïve guide escorted the pair inside. The room was crowded with a dozen renegades; among them was Juan Soto.

Sheriff Morse and Soto locked eyes. Each recognized the other instantly. A long silence, heavy as doom, hung over the room and no one moved. A frieze of desperadoes stood at a bar, holding glasses of whiskey and waiting for the chance to drink the liquid down. The officer next to Morse swallowed hard; every nerve in his body was on alert.

Before any of Soto's men had a chance to assess the situation and react, Sheriff Morse jerked his gun from his holster and leveled it at the outlaw chief. He moved swiftly through the bandits until he was inches away from their leader. Soto carefully raised his hand and motioned for his men to hold their positions. He knew his men could take Morse in an ambush, but not before Morse killed him. Soto's men reluctantly did nothing.

Sheriff Morse ordered Soto to "put up his hands." Soto did as he was told. Morse announced that all of the desperadoes present were under arrest and asked the lawman with him to handcuff Soto.

The deputy moved toward the bandit with every intention of disarming him and placing the cuffs on his hands, but the closer he got to Soto, the more fearful he became. The outlaw stared the lawman down and the deputy slowly started backing up. When the seated Soto slowly pushed his chair away from the table, the deputy turned and ran out of the building.

Sheriff Morse was left alone with the ferocious band of murderers. Suddenly a heavyset woman leapt onto his back and grabbed his pistol arm. One of Soto's gang members grabbed Morse's other arm and Soto jumped to his feet. Pulling his own weapon from his gun belt, he yelled for his men to overpower the sheriff.

Morse's reaction to the command was fast and fluid. Using his considerable strength and agility, he managed to break the hold both people had on him and get off a shot at Soto. His bullet barely missed the bandit's head and struck his hat. Just as the room was erupting in a hail of gunfire, Sheriff Morse sprang backward through the door.

Soto followed after Morse and the battle continued outside. Shots rained down from all directions and from outlaws and lawmen alike. Morse and Soto took cover behind the houses and in the corral. Soto's men, who knew their leader was a deadly shot, shouted for him to kill the sheriff.

The savage renegade answered their request by stepping out into the open with his guns blazing. Bullets rushed past Soto, slamming into doorframes, rain barrels, and nearby trees. Morse watched the bandit make his way toward him. The sheriff was pinned down between a cluster of boulders and a stable of horses. A tremendous fusillade echoed around the lawman.

In a sudden burst of shear fearlessness, Sheriff Morse rose up and ran at his opponent. Both men fired their weapons. When they were within five yards of one another, Soto fired point blank at the sheriff four times, but Morse, with an almost superhuman intuition, timed his shots and dropped to the ground at the precise moment, avoiding Soto's bullets.

Sheriff Harris of Santa Clara, who witnessed the encounter, described it as a "spectacle he would never forget." "The shots were fired in quick succession," Harris later told newspaper reporters. "Soto advancing on Morse every time he fired, with a leap or bound, with pistol held above his head, and as he landed on his feet bringing his weapon to a level with Morse's breast and then firing. After firing he never moved until he had re-cocked his pistol, when tiger-like, he sprang at Morse again.

"I thought Morse was surely hit for his body went almost to the ground, but quick as a flash he sprang erect and returned every shot."

Amidst the smoke and confusion of the scene, Soto decided to run to his horse, which was waiting for him under a tree. The horse became spooked by the incessant gunfire and when Soto tried to mount him, he galloped away. Soto started to run after the animal when he heard the sound of a rifle being cocked.

"Throw down your pistols, Juan," Sheriff Morse demanded, his gun pointing at the bandit's head. "There's been enough shooting." Soto ignored the sheriff and started after another horse. Morse took aim with his rifle and shot the fleeing outlaw in the shoulder. The bullet didn't stop Soto, it only infuriated him more. He turned to the sheriff again and rushed at him firing his guns.

"Never shall I forget," Sheriff Harris remembered later, "how he looked during that terrible encounter, with his long, black hair streaming in the wind, his evil countenance livid with rage and a cocked revolver in each hand."

Before Soto reached the sheriff, Morse brought his carbine rifle to his cheek, stared down the end of the barrel, and shot Soto in the head. Soto staggered a bit, crumbled awkwardly to his knees, and toppled over. The outlaw was dead before he hit the ground.

Henry Plummer

Lawman Gone Bad

Marshal Henry Plummer wiped the tears from Lucinda Vedder's face and gently kissed her bruised lips. She brushed the dark hair off his forehead and forced a smile. "Don't worry," he assured her. "I won't let him hurt you anymore." He eased her up from her chair, pulled her into his lap, and held her close.

The sound of hurried footsteps coming up the outside stairs forced the pair to their feet. Henry pushed his lover out of the way and pulled his six-gun out of his holster. Lucinda's husband, John Vedder, burst through the door, furious. John was a gambler with a short fuse. He and Lucinda were renting their house in Nevada City, California, from Henry. John had suspected that his wife was having an affair with the marshal, but she always denied it. He couldn't beat the truth out of her either. Now, standing in his kitchen, he was face to face with the fact.

"I saw you come here, Plummer. You snake." John snarled. "So what are you going to do?" Henry snapped back. "Your time has come," John barked. He quickly drew his pistol and shot twice at Henry, missing him both times. The marshal smiled and before John could get off another shot, he fired his weapon, hitting him in the shoulder. John turned and quickly raced back down the stairs. Henry followed after him unloading his gun into John's back. John fell to the ground, dead. Henry returned his pistol to his holster and walked back into the house. Lucinda looked on, horrified. "What have I done?" she cried. She hurried out the door to John and dropped down beside him, crying uncontrollably. Henry shook his head in disbelief, walked back into the house, and exited through the front door.

This photo may or may not be of the infamous Sheriff Henry Plummer. Very little about the mysterious Plummer can be verified in the historical record. *Courtesy Searls Historical Library.*

Historical records indicate that the twenty-four-year-old Plummer was not well liked in Nevada City, California. He was elected to the post of town marshal in 1857, and in the short time he held that office, he had been implicated in two murders, not including John Vedder's, and a number of Wells Fargo stage robberies. The local authorities were more than happy to place the corrupt Plummer under arrest for shooting Vedder down and were certain of a guilty verdict at his trial.

Henry Plummer's life began far from the California foothills. He was born in 1832 in Washington County, Maine. The men in his family were sea captains. Henry suffered from consumption and could not follow in their footsteps. His parents made sure he got a good education and hoped he would become a powerful, respected business owner. Henry chose instead to head west to the gold fields and become a miner.

Henry arrived in San Francisco in May 1851. He worked the creeks around Sutter's Fort, but he was never able to find any gold. After a few months he was penniless. He took a job in a bookstore and after a year had saved enough money to buy a ranch and a mine in Nevada County. A year later, he traded his mine shares for a bakery business in Nevada City. He also purchased a few homes and rented them out to pioneer families. Fellow merchants who were impressed with his business integrity persuaded him to run for the position of town marshal. He won the election by a mere seven votes.

While in office Henry showed an amazing aptitude for finding and arresting criminals no one else could locate. Once in jail these criminals had a way of breaking out rather quickly. For a hefty fee above his regular pay as marshal, Henry promised to go after the lawbreakers and bring them back to jail. His ability to recapture all those who escaped, made the county sheriff W. W. Wright and a deputy, David Johnson, suspicious. They publicly voiced their doubts about Henry and shared their theory about the marshal's alleged corruption with anyone who would listen.

Wright and Johnson believed Henry let the prisoners escape so he could earn more money recapturing them. They believed he split the money with his deputies who were keeping an eye on the criminals as they made their getaway. Since the criminals were under constant surveillance, Henry could easily apprehend them and bring them back to justice.

One such outlaw Henry arrested, and who later escaped, was Jim Webster. Webster was a murderer and a thief. Henry claimed to have information that the escaped prisoner might be in an area known as Gold Flat. Sheriff Wright, Deputy Sheriff Johnson, and three other Wright deputies insisted on accompanying Henry and his sidekick Bruce Garvey when they went to get Webster. Henry was offended, but he agreed.

Under the blanket of night, the posse rode out of town. The moon had risen and shadows from a thick canopy of trees and bush made it difficult to see anything clearly. Henry managed to lead the group to a cabin by a small stream where Webster was believed to be hiding out. Webster and his gang heard the lawmen ride up and opened fire.

In the confusion the posse separated. Henry and Bruce went one way, Wright and his men another. Pistol shots were coming from all directions. In the end Webster got away and Sheriff Wright and Deputy Sheriff Johnson, as well as two of Sheriff Wright's deputies, were shot and killed. Henry was accused of leading the sheriff and his deputies into an ambush, a charge he categorically denied.

By the time Henry stood trial for killing John Vedder, his reputation had been soiled. It was almost impossible to find twelve jurors in Nevada County who had not formed an opinion about the marshal's guilt. After several months of searching, a full jury was finally selected.

Lucinda Vedder testified that her husband was abusive toward her and that he instigated the shoot-out between himself and Plummer. Witnesses at the scene claimed no gun was found on or around John's body when they saw him lying dead at the foot of the stairs. That damaging information, the fact that Henry was having an affair with a married woman, and the testimony from local citizens about the marshal's questionable character helped bring about a guilty verdict.

Henry was sentenced to ten years at San Quentin. Once inside he befriended a prison physician who testified that Henry was dying of consumption. Henry's attorney began a successful campaign to get his ailing client out of jail. Six months after Henry entered prison, the governor issued him a full pardon and he was released.

Disgraced and bitter, Henry returned to Nevada City, his illness miraculously in remission. He was hired on as a policeman, and shortly after being sworn in, he arrested an escaped convict from San Quentin. Like so many of Henry's detainees, the convict broke out of jail. Henry was fired and for a while drifted from job to job, always working in the mining fields.

On February 12, 1861, Henry was having a drink at a brothel when he noticed escaped convict, Bill Riley, talking with a prostitute. Henry attempted to make a citizen's arrest. Riley resisted and the two fought. According to the newspaper, the *Nevada County Democrat*, what happened next sealed Henry's fate in the Gold Country.

"It appears that Henry Plummer and William Riley had both been drinking pretty freely, and had got to quarreling, when Riley struck Plummer on the head with a knife, cutting through his hat and inflicting a deep wound in the scalp. Plummer at the same time drew a revolver and fired at Riley. The ball took effect in his left side and must have killed him instantly. Plummer was taken into custody and lodged in jail."

Police officials agreed that Plummer had acted in self-defense, but fearing that his prison record would prevent a fair trial, they counseled him to leave the area and then allowed him to walk away from the jail. For a time Plummer roamed about Nevada, teaming up with gamblers and fugitives from justice. Henry and his men robbed stages and Wells Fargo offices and killed three men before drifting into Idaho.

Although Plummer was a thief, he behaved like a peace officer. While working in a gambling casino in Lewiston, Idaho, he rounded up a gang of outlaws and ordered the killing of the head of a vigilante committee that was going to hang the bandits. After the man was stabbed and decapitated, Henry recruited the frightened vigilantes into his gang.

Plummer was a powerful man, but not as the respected business owner his parents had hoped he would become. He was wanted for crimes committed in three states. He was disheartened by the way his life turned out and felt that his career in the West was over. Hoping to make a fresh start, he decided to return to his childhood home in Maine. Hot on his trail was a bounty hunter named Jack Cleveland. Cleveland befriended Henry, telling him he was a horse trader from California. The two rode together to Fort Benton, Montana, where Henry was to catch a steamer headed east.

While the two were there, an agent of a nearby government farm hurried into the fort, begging for volunteers to defend his family against an anticipated Indian attack. Henry and Jack joined the fight and helped drive the Indians out of the area. When the fighting was over, the men decided to stay on for a while and make sure the town was indeed safe. By this time Jack and Henry had become good friends. Jack decided against turning Henry over to the authorities and collecting the reward.

At a dance one evening, the pair was introduced to a beautiful woman named Electa Bryan who was residing at the fort and both fell hopelessly in love with her. When Electa fell in love with Henry, Jack vowed to get even and to make good on his original plan to bring him in. Henry was inspired by Electa's love for him and was convinced that with her as his wife he could overcome any challenge.

On hearing the news of the latest gold discovery in Bannack, Montana, Henry decided to leave his fiancée and pursue his fortune. This time he was sure he would find gold. The resentful Jack rode along with him, intent on overtaking Henry once they reached their destination.

On January 14, 1863, Jack Cleveland was with his friend Hank Crawford at Bannock's Goodrich Hotel and Saloon. The two were talking and flirting with the prostitutes who worked there. Jack loaded up on whiskey and told Hank all about Henry's past sins and how he was going to collect a handsome reward for the outlaw. When Henry wandered

42

into the saloon for a drink, the intoxicated bounty hunter attempted to provoke a fight.

Henry was stunned to learn who Jack really was and tried to talk him out of turning him over to the authorities. Jack went for his gun. Henry drew his pistol and fired a warning shot into the saloon ceiling, but Jack wouldn't back down. Three times he went for his revolver, and three times, before he could get off a shot, he took a bullet from Henry's gun. Jack fell down dead, still clutching his weapon.

Henry was arrested and later acquitted when a miner's jury determined he acted in self-defense. Five months later those same miners elected him as sheriff of Bannack and of all the surrounding area. Town officials said, "No man stood higher in the estimation of the community than Henry Plummer."

Before riding back to Fort Benton to marry his beloved Electa, the newly elected sheriff organized a deputy network throughout the camps. Many of Henry's deputies were thieves and outlaws who used to ride with him. They called themselves the Innocents, and they had secret handshakes and code words to recognize one another from the imposters who wanted to join the gang.

When Henry returned to Bannack with his new bride, he promised to make up for his past shortcoming by tracking down anyone who broke the law. Henry ordered his deputies to round up all the criminals they could find and hang them on the spot. They were also ordered to hang anyone who stood in the way of acting out the Innocents' brand of justice.

Henry and his men would separate the outlaws they lynched from the gold and money those outlaws had stolen and share the profits. They also divided up the gold from shipments they intercepted, being carried by the stages that traveled from the mines to the banks. The Innocents killed more than one hundred men and became the most powerful force in the territory. The ambitious sheriff soon extended his operations to Virginia City, Montana, and forced the lawmen there out of business.

Hank Crawford, Jack Cleveland's friend and confidant, and now resident of Virginia City, began telling his fellow citizens what he knew about Henry's corrupt past. Henry drove Hank out of town and Hank was never heard from again. What he had to say about the sheriff did not fall on deaf ears, however. Virginia City and Bannack residents already suspicious of Sheriff Plummer formed their own vigilance committee.

One by one the vigilance committee captured members of the Innocents. The men were strung up, but not before being forced to give out the names of others in their gang. Red Yeager, one of Henry's deputies, admitted that the sheriff was the leader of the Innocents. The committee was stunned by the confession. Finally, their suspicions were confirmed.

"That's right," Red said. "Henry Plummer! He's fooled plenty of people, but he's the chief. You'll find out I'm right." Yeager went on to tell the committee about all of the Innocents' misdeeds, including minor robberies and holdups. When Yeager was through talking, he was hanged from a cottonwood tree. Before they left the spot the vigilantes fastened a placard to the coat of the dead man that read, RED! ROAD AGENT AND MESSENGER FOR THE INNOCENTS. The vigilantes of Montana hanged all the Innocents they were able to catch.

Although word was out that the committee had their sights set on Henry, he made no attempt to leave the area. He had made a deal with some of the members of the vigilantes and was convinced he was not in any danger.

Some of the vigilante members eventually double-crossed him, and on January 10, 1864, Sheriff Henry Plummer was taken into custody.

Henry was marched to the pine gallows he himself had built. Crying and begging for mercy, the former lawman pleaded that they cut out his tongue, hack off all his limbs, and leave him in his cabin in the hills. No one took his suggestion and he was hanged. His obituary, found in the *Aura California Times*, colorfully outlined the life of the sheriff who ended up a villain.

"Henry Plummer was a young man, small in stature, of prepossessing appearance, and of fair education. He had energy, ability and business tact, sufficient to have made him a useful citizen and an honorable member of society. But that terrible course which has taken possession of so many young men on the Pacific Coast, the desire to be considered a desperado and fighting man, was the ruin of him. He had killed two men at least and shot and stabbed a number of others.

"When the last hour arrived in his reckless career, and the shadow of death flitted before his eyes, Plummer is said to have weakened. His fortitude gave way and he cried like a child. We doubt not that in the bitterness of despair he exclaimed, as did one of the unfortunate young men who met death on the scaffold last week in this city, 'O, God! That I had another life to live!'"

Charles Earl "Black Bart" Boles
What Rhymes with Crime?

The Arena Stage slowly plodded along the rocky road over a mountain pass en route to Duncan Mills, California. It had been a bumpy, dusty commute for the passengers inside. The driver followed the worn ruts in the path in an attempt to make the ride more comfortable, but the falling rocks from the hillside that had lodged themselves into the grooves made a smooth ride impossible. The August sun blasted down through the trees, adding intense heat to the unpleasant travel mix. The last few miles to the stage stop felt like a hundred.

Suddenly the horses were spooked and reared back. The driver pulled on the reins of the team and jerked the stage to a halt. A sinister-looking figure stepped out from behind a massive oak tree. It was a man dressed in a long, dirty-white duster, a fine tailored pair of trousers, shirt, and jacket. He wore a flour sack over his head, with holes cut out for the eyes, and flour sacks covered his feet and were tied at the ankles. The man leveled a double-barreled shotgun at the driver.

Casting a glance around, the nervous teamster spotted what appeared to be several guns pointing at him from behind nearby rocks and trees. As if to dissuade the driver from considering reaching for his weapon in a moment of bravery, the bandit called out, "If he dares to shoot, give him a solid volley, boys."

The thief motioned at the strongbox under the driver's seat with his gun. "Sure hope you have a lot of gold in that box," the man grinned. "I'm nearly out of money." The driver studied the outlaw for a moment then reached down, grabbed the box, and held it in his lap. "Please throw down the box," the bandit ordered. The driver did as he was told and tossed the strongbox, filled with several hundred dollars in gold, onto the ground. The thief quickly grabbed the box and disappeared into the woods. The stunned passengers looked on, not daring to move. The driver grabbed the reins of the team and spurred the horses out of the area.

Highwayman Black Bart removed the flour sack from his head and watched the stage vanish from sight in a trail of dust. He smiled to himself as he emptied the strongbox. Inside was $300 in cash and $300 in checks. He removed a piece of paper from the pocket of his duster and dropped it into the empty coffer. "A little something for the law," he chuckled to himself. Black Bart then raced off into the trees. The posse that would soon be hot on his trail eventually found the note that told something of the history of the lone bandit and explained his motives:

> I've labored long and hard for bread,
> For honor and for riches,
> But on my corns too long you've tred,
> You fine-haired sons-of-bitches.

Black Bart held up more than two dozen stages during his eight-year career as an expert lone bandit in the California foothills. He was born Charles Earl Boles in Norfolk County, England, in 1829. He was the seventh of nine children born to his parents, John and Maria. When Charles was two, his father moved the family to Jefferson County, New York. There the Boles family worked a homestead of a hundred acres, farming and raising livestock. By the time Charles was twenty, he had had his fill of farm life. He was ambitious and wanted to see the world.

In 1849 Charles set out for the gold fields of California with dreams of striking it rich. He had some success mining for gold along the American River, but the life of a miner was rough. Standing in ice-cold streams in search of nuggets, sifting through pans of gravel, braving the elements, feasting on moldy biscuits, and long, lonely nights were more than the discouraged Charles had anticipated. His younger brother, Robert, followed him to the Gold Country in 1852. Charles's spirits

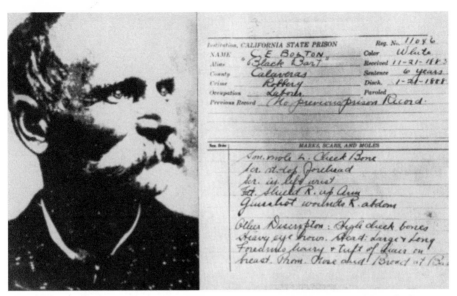

The outlaw known as "Black Bart" often left verses describing his crimes for law enforcement to find. *Courtesy of Searls Historical Library.*

were lifted by his brother's company, but this improvement was short lived. Robert took ill and died after having been in California for only eight months.

Brokenhearted and through with mining, Charles left the area and headed home. One the way back to New York, he stopped in Decatur, Illinois. There he met Mary Elizabeth Johnson and fell in love. The couple married, and by 1861 Mary had given Charles two girls. Charles was a family man now, but he remained restless. The security of hearth and home did not offer the fortune or excitement he craved.

The nation was at war and Charles decided to join the fight. He enlisted for three years with the 116th Illinois Infantry. He participated in the siege of Vicksburg and Jackson and was with William Tecumseh Sherman during the campaign in the Carolinas.

On May 26, 1864, he was severely wounded during a march into Georgia. He was discharged from the service shortly thereafter. He returned home to his wife and children; purchased a few acres of land in New Oregon, Iowa; and began farming. The lifestyle proved to be unsatisfying for Charles and he resolved to search for an alternative way of making a living.

By 1867 Charles was on his way to conquer the gold and silver mines scattered across the wild frontier. He wrote his wife from a prospector's camp in Silver Bow, Montana, in August of 1871 and informed her that he was headed to California. After accepting the fact that he would never be a prosperous miner, historians speculate Boles decided to teach school in Contra Costa and Sierra County, California. His income as an educator was meager, and within four years time, he had abandoned the profession in favor of becoming a thief. Convinced he could make more money as a criminal than a legitimate businessman, Boles chose to start robbing stagecoaches. On July, 26, 1875, he held up a wagon carrying $160 in gold notes. It was the first of more than two dozen robberies he orchestrated in his career.

Mary Elizabeth had no idea what had become of her nomadic husband. He had stopped writing her in 1872 and she assumed he had died.

Boles used the name "Black Bart" whenever he was stealing from stages. The well-read bandit borrowed the name from the main character in his favorite novel, *The Case of Summerfield*. Written by San Francisco attorney William H. Rhodes, the story was centered around a desperate man who had a secret weapon that could destroy the entire world. Boles thought of himself as being just as desperate as the subject in the book and took the handle on as his own.

Many of Boles's daring robberies took place at night and involved not only the theft of Wells Fargo gold shipments, but also mail being carried from mining camp to mining camp. Oftentimes the letters contained money that Boles pocketed. It was a one-man operation, but Boles planned each crime to make it appear as though there were several men involved. He would place sticks that resembled guns behind rocks and trees and call out to his wooden gang during the holdup. He made his getaway on foot and always wore gunny sacks over his boots so he wouldn't leave any heel marks in the dirt to be followed.

Between 1875 and 1883, Black Bart robbed twenty-eight stages and collected more than $18,000. From the first holdup, county sheriffs and deputies investigating the robberies were baffled. For a time the only clue ever found at the scene of the crime was the occasional poem penned by the perpetrator.

Law enforcement's inability to apprehend the frustrated poet-bandit led many miners to speculate that the criminal was a ghost. Dime store novels were written about the mysterious robber, raising his popularity to mythical proportions.

Black Bart's robbery of Wells Fargo stages were sporadic. He would go as long as nine months between holdups. He told stage drivers, "I only take what's needed, when it's needed." Most teamsters were submissive and seldom defied the bandit, obediently tossing him the strongbox when ordered to do so.

Wells Fargo detective James B. Hume was determined to catch Black Bart and put an end to his actions no matter how polite or considerate the thief pretended to be. He thoroughly investigated every scene and issued the first wanted poster for the outlaw. The initial price on Bart's head was $250 and one-fourth of any stolen money recovered.

In between holdups Black Bart passed himself off as a miner going to and from his claim. He even carried a few raw nuggets to make the act more believable. He was welcomed at remote ranches he passed and worked hard for the room and board he was offered.

From time to time he would leave the mountains behind and travel to San Francisco. He frequented theaters and bookstores dressed in tailor-made tweed suits, a bowler hat, and topcoat, while carrying a cane. Combined with his gray hair and moustache, pale-blue eyes, and lanky frame, Boles left acquaintances in the mining towns and cities with the impression that he was a success.

On July 25, 1878, the slick, well-coifed desperado orchestrated the robbery of the Quincy-Oroville stage. He took an expensive diamond ring and cash from the passengers and more than $350 from the onboard safe. He left another poem behind which read,

Here I lay me down to sleep
To wait the coming morrow,
Perhaps success, perhaps defeat,
And everlasting sorrow.
Let come what will I'll try it on,
My condition can't be worse;
And if there's money in that box
'Tis money in my purse.
Black Bart
the PO8.

Authorities carefully analyzed the note and determined that each line had been penned in a different hand. The reward for information that would lead officials to the poem's author and the identity of "PO8" increased to $8,000.

After Black Bart's twelfth robbery in October of 1878, the gentlemanly desperado learned he had made what could have been a crucial mistake. He had been spotted the day before around the location of the holdup. But Boles's cunning and willingness to lay low after realizing his blunder kept police at bay for another four years.

Problems apart from being seen and staying ahead of law enforcement erupted in the summer of 1882. Black Bart's luck with dutiful drivers came to an abrupt end. On July 13, he stopped a stage outside of the town of Strawberry, California, and politely asked the teamsters to throw the strongbox off the stage. The driver reached for his rifle and fired at the criminal. Black Bart hurried off into the woods, but not before being grazed in the side by a bullet. He recovered quickly and by September was back at work.

Again he met with an uncooperative driver who fired a shot at him as he was dragging the strongbox into the brush. This time the bullet struck Charles in the left wrist, and he used one of his handkerchiefs to wrap around the wound. During his quick getaway he dropped the handkerchief, leaving behind a valuable clue for detectives to find. On careful inspection the officers found a laundry mark on the material. It was traced back to a business in San Francisco. The detectives visited ninety-one laundries in the city trying to track down Black Bart.

After a weeklong search they were able to match the markings on the handkerchief with the mark on the books at the American Laundry. When they questioned the business owner about the hanky, he told them the property belonged to C. E. Bolton, a respectable mine engineer. Law enforcement officers were able to secure an address for their suspect and immediately set out to make an arrest.

Detective Hume elicited the cooperation of a shop owner who knew Black Bart to positively identify him. Hume and his men waited outside the outlaw's hotel, and as soon as Bart approached the building, the shop owner pointed him out. He was arrested moments later. When Black Bart's room was searched, a partially written letter in the same hand as the notes left behind at the stage robberies was found. The criminal scoffed at the idea that there was any connection between himself and the stage robber, and when he was booked into jail, he claimed his name was T. Z. Spaulding.

After several days of denying he was Black Bart, Boles finally broke down and admitted who he really was. In exchange for pleading guilty to one of the twenty-eight robberies and avoiding a trial, he was given a reduced sentence of six years. The judge ordered him to serve out his time at the San Quentin Prison. He was fifty-four years old.

Shortly after his prison term started, he began writing letters to his wife and their grown-up daughters. Charles was completely demoralized by his incarceration and searched for the right words to explain the path he had taken.

"Oh my dear family, how little you know of the terrible ordeal I have passed through, and how few if what the world calls good men are worth the giant powder it would take to blow them into eternity. Thousands in every day life that would be called good, nice men, are until the circumstances change them and give them a chance to show their real character."

Black Bart was released from prison on January 21, 1888. He had been a model prisoner who provided a valuable service in the facilities dispensary. His sentenced was reduced by more than a year and a half because of good behavior. Time in jail had aged the gentlemen outlaw. He was deaf in one ear and was losing his eyesight. Reporters swarmed around him as he walked out of the prison gates. "You plan on robbing anymore stagecoaches, Black Bart?" one reporter asked.

"No gentlemen," Bart quickly replied, "I'm all through with crime."

"Will you be writing any more poetry?" another reporter asked.

"Young man, didn't you hear me say I would commit no more crimes?" he laughed.

Black Bart was an unsettled man outside of prison. He stayed on in San Francisco for a time contemplating what to do next. He continued to write warm, affectionate letters to his wife, but his future plans were vague. It is clear from his letters home that he had no intentions of returning to Mary anytime soon.

"Oh, my constant loving Mary and my children, I did hope and had good reason for hoping to be able to come to you and end all this terrible uncertainty, but it seems it will end only in my life. Although I am free and in fair health, I am most miserable. My dear family, I wish you would give me up forever and be happy, for I feel I shall be a burden to you as I live no matter where I am. My loving family, I would willing[ly] sacrifice my life to enjoy your loving company for a single week as I once was. I fear you blame me for not coming, but Heaven knows it is an utter impossibility."

Law enforcement officials kept a close eye on Bart after his release, but he never traveled far from San Francisco, and as time went by, the police became lax in their surveillance of the bandit. Black Bart eventually drifted out of the Bay Area and headed southwest toward Modesto.

By March 1889, Black Bart seemed to have vanished, leaving behind a only a few personal possessions at a hotel in Visalia to prove he ever existed. Detectives suspected the outlaw had come out of retirement when a Wells Fargo stage was robbed in November. The thief had left a note that read,

> So here I've stood while wind and rain
> Have set the trees a-sobbin'
> And risked my life for that damned box,
> That wasn't worth the robbin'.

Detective Hume declared the note a hoax and the work of a copycat bandit.

The whereabouts of Black Bart could not be determined by law enforcement agencies and his legend grew. Writers and reporters continued to "find" Black Bart living in a hundred different places and robbing stages until Wells Fargo decided to close its last stage route in 1895. It was also rumored that Bart died in the California mountains while hunting wild game. What really became of the poet outlaw has never been discovered.

Jesús Tejada
Caught Napping

Jesús Tejada and two members of his outlaw gang studied the exterior of a general store at a stage stop twenty miles from Stockton, California. Looking in through the clean glass windows that covered the front of the building, Tejada watched the clerk showing costumers around the tidy, well-stocked business.

Tejada's face was set in a scowl as he dismounted his horse and tied the animal's reins to a hitching post. He had deep-set dark eyes in a rough-carved face, and his black hair hung down across his forehead. His hands were thick and scarred. He was twenty-four years old, but the menacing expression he wore made him look ten years older.

Tejada's men followed the desperado inside the store, and after being in the brilliance of the sunshine, they squinted against the shadowy interior. The four shoppers milling about the store looked up from their potential purchases and watched the heavily armed thugs separate and take positions at various points around them. The uneasy clerk timidly approached Tejada and asked him if he could be of any help.

"I'm here to take it all, señor," Tejada said without smiling. "Take it?" The clerk replied. "I don't understand." Tejada removed his pistol from his gun belt and pointed it at the man's head. "I think you do," Tejada said coolly. Without flinching he shot the clerk in the face. Then his men opened fire on the customers. When the smoke cleared, five innocent people were dead on the floor. Tejada ordered the bandits in his charge to stack the victims in the corner like a cord of wood. They accomplished their gruesome task while Tejada emptied the cash register of its contents and helped himself to the supplies on the shelf.

The Stockton area was the scene of the brutal crimes of Jesús Tejada in 1887.
Courtesy of California History Section, California State Library.

The desperadoes rode off into the setting sun, their saddlebags bulging with merchandise and cash.

Jesús Tejada's reign of outlaw terror extended over a little more than two-year period from late 1885 to early 1888. He was a highwayman and murderer who explained away his vicious actions as being a response to the overwhelming number of white settlers in the region who were unwilling to give him legitimate work. He managed to frustrate numerous attempts by law enforcement to apprehend him and his criminal entourage. It wasn't until the former sheriff of Alameda County, Harry Morse, joined the search for the renegade that Tejada was finally brought down.

There is little in the historical record concerning Jesús Tejada. It is impossible to confirm where he was born or his exact date of birth. Harry Morse wrote a great deal about the outlaw and his quest to bring the man to trial. According to the lawman, Tejada had been born in 1864 in the San Joaquin Valley.

On the other hand, the last days of Tejada's life and the major crime that led to his demise are well documented. After the December 12, 1887, killings of the store clerk and patrons, a posse was formed to track the outlaw and his gang down. Morse was asked by state authorities to help in the search. He had retired from the sheriff's office in 1878 and was the owner of a San Francisco–based detective agency. His knowledge of the terrain and previous experience helping to bring in such bad men as Juan Soto and Black Bart prompted the law enforcement community to tap into his expertise.

Morse and several deputies pursued Tejada vigorously for weeks before a former rider with the outlaw named Luis led them to the location of the bandit. The search for Tejada ended on January 1, 1888.

Morse's account of the event, which appeared in the *San Francisco Morning Call* on January 7, 1888, described the anxious moments leading to his arrest.

> Besides Tejada there were six other Mexicans hiding in the camp. Tejada and three others slept under a large oak tree that grew near the hut of a man named José Maria. He occupied the hut with his woman, while old Patrick Mencillos (one of Tejada's friends) slept on the main trail about fifty yards below, where the others were sleeping and acted as sentinels.
>
> It was arranged that we would retire early and get as much rest as possible, get up at 1 o'clock in the morning, have Luis [Luis is also referred to as Lew by Sheriff Morse] drive us to the mouth of the canyon and leave us there, he to return to the ranch where we made our way up to Jose Marias's camp and attempted the arrest, doing as best we could under the circumstances. At one in the morning we were up and ready to start. It was a cold, dreary and blustering morning, the wind swept down through the mountain

pass—a perfect hurricane. The strong gust of wind tore through the telegraph wires that were strung along in front of the rancho and gave out sweet musical sounds as of an English harp.

"Whew," said Luis, "how the winds do blow." We drove silently toward the canyon. Each one of us seemed to be lost in thought; the others of us thinking, no doubt—as I certainly was—about how the thing would end, and not knowing but that in a few hours one of us might not be in the land of believing.

As we drew near the place where Luis was to leave us, the late moon commenced to rise over the top of the eastern hills, throwing its silvery rays and making dark shadows across the little valleys and making the surrounding country more discernible. Luis drew up at a bunch of willows near the canyon and we got out ready to start on foot to our objective point. We bade Luis return to the rancho and to expect us there by noon. If not there by that time to summon assistance and come to our relief.

Up the steep mountain we started. A half hour hard trudging brought us to the ridge. Turning to the left we walked cautiously along for about two miles, and until we got as best I could judge, opposite the corral near Jose Maria's hut. . . ."

Sheriff Morse and his men were awoken before dawn and began making plans to advance on Tejada's camp. Luis warned the lawmen not to alarm the desperadoes' dogs because the animals' barking could give away their location. Morse assured Luis that they could avoid the dogs if they climbed the mountain pass behind the cabins and snuck down to the hideout via the ravines in the canyon. "The late moon was a grand thing for us," Morse recounted later. "It enabled us to distinguish objects quite clearly. We commenced to crawl carefully down the little ravine toward the corral . . . ." The posse crept over the dry, rugged terrain as quietly as they could. Every pebble that slid loose and every twig that snapped under their feet caused them to stop and wait. They pressed on only after they were certain the bandits had not heard their slow approach. "At last we reached the end of the ravine and emerged into the main canyon," Morse remembered. "Looking about we discovered the old corral about fifty yards above us. Crawling along on our hands and knees we were soon alongside of it. Here for a few moments we rested and fixed between ourselves our plan of attack. We were within a hundred yards of the whole gang and they were sound asleep, not suspecting for a moment that an enemy was so close upon them.

"From what Luis had told us we knew that old Patricio was lying on the trail between us and the hut and it was necessary to capture him before he could send the alarm to those who occupied it. Our plan was to run quickly by him and surprise the others in their sleep. I was to hold the gang undercover of my Winchester, while Lew [Luis] handcuffed Tejada. Then he was to march down the canyon with the prisoner while I covered the retreat." Morse and his men held their position until the sun arose. A half an hour after daylight they made their move.

"All being ready, we each stripped off the heavy overcoats we were wearing and laid them down beside the corral," Sheriff Morse relayed later. "Throwing a cartridge into my gun, we stepped out from beside the corral into the trail and made directly for old Patrick. In a second we were beside him. He awoke with a start, sat up, rubbed his eyes and looked at as—that is, he looked into the muzzle of a six-shooter. I stooped down and whispered into his ear that if he made the least noise we would blow the top of his head off and told him as long as he kept perfectly still he was safe, but the least alarm made by him to the others would be the signal for his death. All he said was 'Bueno, señor,' and fell back into his blankets again and covered up his head."

After capturing the outpost and some of Tejada's sleeping men, Sheriff Morse and his deputies moved in on the bandit's main army.

"In a second more we were in the midst of the camp and got a cross-fire drop on them before they knew we were there," Morse recalled. "A quick stern command from me for them to hold up their hands had a most magical effect, and brought every one of them into a sitting position with each of them holding his hands high above his head.

"I told Tejada to get up and come to us. He seemed rather slow to obey, but a sharp, 'Pronto, pronto, señor,' and at the same time pointing the rifle directly at his head, had the desired effect and we soon had him handcuffed and on his way down the canyon."

After collecting their coats at the corral, Sheriff Morse and his posse quickly ushered Tejada out of the area. They followed along the edge of a creek until they reached the main road and began the nine mile walk to the San Luis Ranch where Luis was awaiting their arrival. The posse camped that evening on the banks of the San Joaquin River. Sheriff Morse stayed close to Tejada. The desperadoes attempted to lay hold of a piece of wood to use to hit the Sheriff over the head, but Morse managed to stop him. The lawman then handcuffed Tejada's right wrist to his left one and they settled down to sleep. Ranch hands and their families stopped working and stared in amazement at the prisoner as he was escorted onto the ranch the following day.

"At daybreak we were on the road again and a drive of twenty miles brought us to Bantas, a station on the line of the Central Pacific Railroad," Sheriff Morse recounted later. "There I took the train with the prisoner. . . . The next day I took Tejada to Stockton and delivered him to the authorities of San Joaquin County. Tejada was indicted, tried and convicted of the multiple murders and sentenced to be hanged.

Jesús Tejada never made it to the gallows. He died of natural causes in jail soon after the trial and conviction.

Juan Flores
He Took a Short Fall

Four teams of tired, uninspired horses pulled a line of buckboards filled with coffins over the dry, dusty terrain twelve miles outside of the village of San Juan Capistrano. The wagon drivers and a dozen other men riding with them stared soberly out at the land. Ahead in the near distance they could see a smattering of dead bodies strewn across the semidesert floor. Misshapen dead horses, bloating in the heat, lay beside their lifeless owners.

As the buckboards inched closer to the carnage, the wheels of the vehicles cut through pools of clotted blood spread over the ground. The drivers slowed the teams to a halt and without speaking the men on board the wagons began unloading the wooden crates. Their busy hands then lifted the bodies off the hard earth and placed them in the coffins.

All of the corpses were wearing badges; five of the men were deputies and one was Los Angeles sheriff James R. Barton. Each of the lawmen was riddled with bullets; they had been stripped of their belongings and their right eyes had been shot out.

The objective of the slain posse, dispatched on January 22, 1857, was to track down a cattle rustler and horse thief named Juan Flores. Flores's criminal activities began in 1855. He had run roughshod over a stretch of Southern California that extended from Sacramento to the San Joaquin Valley. Along the way he recruited more than fifty outlaws to assist him in the looting and killing of ranchers and their families.

When Sheriff Barton learned of Flores's hideout he wasted no time organizing volunteers. The experienced lawman believed he could apprehend the murderous bandit. He had no idea when he was riding

The region around San Juan Capistrano was home to Juan Flores and his gang.
Courtesy of California History Section, California State Library.

hard toward the area where Flores was last seen that he was riding into an ambush.

Once the sheriff's body and those of his deputies were secured in the coffins, the boxes were stacked inside the buckboards. Another posse was sent out to find Flores and bring him to justice, now not only for his existing sins, but also for the brutal slaying of Barton and his men. The search for Flores was one of the largest manhunts in Old West history.

Juan Flores was born in 1835 in Santa Barbara, California. His parents were well-respected members of the community and proud of the handsome son they believed would grow up to be an exceptional man. It is not known what prompted Flores to abandon the high hopes his mother and father had for him and embark on a life of crime. Historians suggest that the Flores family was a struggling family of farmers and that Juan aspired to a more affluent lifestyle. He was not opposed to achieving his goal illegally either. He left home at seventeen and joined a gang of ruthless cattle rustlers made up of American drifters, Mexican bandits, ex-convicts, fugitives, and army deserters.

Cattle was a critical element of the economy of the West. California-grown beef was used to supply the growing population of prospectors and immigrant families with meat and it increased in price daily. Because of the rising price of beef—and the profits to be made—the territory was infested with bands of cattle thieves committing depredations upon the ranges. Ranchers not only had to worry about bandits stealing from them, but hungry and desperate Native Americans as well. Some cattle owners lost entire herds to either Indians or rustlers.

Flores rode with a bandito bunch that raided cattle farms around the area of Rancho Santa Margarita. He primarily focused on stealing horses and was eventually arrested for the offense in 1856. He was tried and convicted and was ordered to serve his time in the jail at San Quentin. Flores was bitter over his circumstances and restless while confined inside a cell. Anxious to be free, he teamed up with a hundred other inmates in a massive jailbreak. The plans were thwarted before the prisoners were able to flee the premises, however.

Flores was discouraged, but he was not defeated. With the help of several fellow outlaws, his second attempt to break out of prison was a success. The elaborate escape involved overtaking the crew onboard a ship docked at the wharf at Point San Quentin. The inexperienced bandit sailors managed to steer the vessel out of the harbor amidst a barrage of gunfire from prison guards and law enforcement officers. The lawless crew navigated the ship through the open waters, making it to the Contra Costa shoreline where they docked. The men then split up and went their separate ways.

Law enforcement combed the hills around Santa Barbara looking for Flores and the others, but the felons could not be found. Flores had managed to elude the lawmen making his way to San Luis Obispo.

Once he reached the picturesque town, the ambitious renegade immediately began enlisting a host of like-minded criminals to join him in his illegal ventures.

The most savage of all of Flores's recruits was twenty-year-old Andres Fontes. Fontes claimed he was driven to a life of crime by Sheriff James Barton. The two had been in love with the same woman when Barton accused Fontes of stealing a horse to get rid of him. Fontes spent two years in prison for the alleged theft and vowed to kill Barton when he was released. His hatred for law enforcement and bent toward law-breaking made him a natural to team up with Flores.

Bandits were drawn to Flores's charm and criminal vision. He organized and led more than fifty men on numerous cattle-rustling raids. It was an easy transition from cattle rustling to robbery for Flores. He organized the looting of small towns, stage holdups, and the ransacking of prospectors' camps. He and his men also kidnapped lone travelers and held them for ransom. Dead bodies were oftentimes left in the wake of the mayhem. Residents in mining communities throughout the state were petrified of the fugitive and his gang.

Flores fueled the fear with bold, public acts of violence. In late 1856, the bandit and his gang snatched a German settler off a trail outside of San Diego. They demanded the victim pay a hefty sum for his release, but the settler refused. Flores made an example of the man in the town square. With hundreds looking on, he shot the stubborn immigrant to death.

With the help of his love interest Chola Martina, Flores and his desperadoes invaded the homes and businesses of two well-known mercantile owners in San Juan Capistrano. One of the men was murdered trying to protect his property.

News of the gang's continual vicious attacks prompted Los Angeles sheriff Barton to form a posse and set out after the murderers and thieves. Barton had been informed that Flores's band was some fifty men strong, but he believed that the number had been exaggerated by hysterical crime victims. The sheriff's underestimation of the strength of Flores's gang resulted in his death. One of the men who gunned down Barton was Andres Fontes. At last he had his revenge.

General Don Andres Pico, a prominent Los Angeles land owner and the brother of the last Mexican governor of California, took charge of forming a posse after the slaughter of Barton and his deputies. Pico pulled together a fifty-one-man army of Mexicans and Americans to go after Flores. Pauma Indian leader, Manuelito Cota, in Temecula, joined the general in his efforts. Manuelito recruited forty-three Indians for the task. A group of enraged citizens in the San Diego area made up a third posse out to track Flores down.

Pauma scouts ventured ahead of the posses to look for clues as to where the bandit might have fled. The location of Flores's camp was finally narrowed down to the mountains around El Cariso. With the assistance of one of Flores's former gang members, Pico's Californians, as they were known, were able to find the exact location of Flores's cabin hideout. The Californians attacked the shelter under the light of a full moon. The desperadoes inside fired on the posse killing or wounding many of their pursuers. Some of the bandits were shot while trying to make a run for their horses, others were captured unharmed, and some managed to get away. Juan Flores and Andres Fontes were two who escaped.

Flores and Fontes were lost in the smoke of gunfire and vanished into the tangled mountain thicket. General Pico sent for reinforcements and shortly after his supplies of guns, ammunition, and men were replenished, he continued the pursuit of the outlaws. On February 1, 1857, a faction of the posse, headed by Dr. J. Gentry from Los Angeles, cornered Flores and two of his companions near Santiago Mountain.

The bandits shot it out with the posse members, but realizing they were outnumbered, they surrendered. Flores and his diminished band of followers were escorted to a nearby ranch were they were placed under guard in a weathered adobe building. The prisoners' stay was meant to be temporary. Given Flores's previous success at escaping from his captors, the authorities wanted more law enforcement on hand to escort the criminal to the Los Angeles jail. But in spite of the precautions taken, Flores wriggled out of his cuffs and broke out of the crumbling, clay holding cell.

Posse members' tempers flared at the news that Flores had gotten away. General Pico ordered his deputies to immediately put to death the members of Flores's gang that were arrested with him. Pico then helped enlist more than 120 men to join the manhunt to find Juan Flores. For eleven days one of the largest posses ever assembled in the Old West searched the territory along the Los Angeles River between San Juan Capistrano and Temecula.

Almost twenty-four hours after Flores had escaped, he was stopped by two armed sentinels patrolling the grounds at a Simi Valley ranch. He lied about his identity, but his suspicious behavior led the guards to take him to the ranch owner to be questioned further. The land baron recognized the bandit and informed his men that the scoundrel in custody was none other than Juan Flores.

Flores was taken to Los Angeles where he was tried and sentenced to death. After his trial ended on February 14, 1857, a hostile crowd surrounded the jail demanding the notorious outlaw be turned over to them. They wanted Flores hanged at that moment. On February 21, the criminal was turned over to the enraged mob and they led him to the gallows.

Before the noose was placed around his neck, the twenty-two-year-old Flores's arms and legs were bound and his eyes were covered with a white handkerchief. He whispered a few last words and then the trap door was sprung. He did not die instantly. The fall was shorter than planned and the rope was a bit too long. After a gruesome six-minute struggle it was over.

"Rattlesnake Dick" Barter
No Jail Could Hold Him

The hot wind howled through the shrieking forest like a troop of demons around the Trinity Mountains between Yreka and San Francisco. Four masked men waited in the shadows of the massive oak trees for a mule-drawn stagecoach lumbering along a rugged path. The Wells Fargo carriage was carrying more than $80,000 worth of gold shipped from the rich mining communities in Shasta County to the crowded City by the Bay. An armed convoy of six guards surrounded the shipment. Their eyes were fixed on the wooded area that lined the trail. As the mules pulled the heavy vehicle through a rocky ravine a shot rang out. One of the guards toppled off the back of his spooked horse with a bullet hole in his chest. The abrupt disturbance caused the mules to buck and squirm and the driver tried desperately to regain control of the frightened team. Another gunshot rang out and a second fatally injured guard was thrown from the saddle.

In a few quick moments the ruthless outlaws had overtaken the stage. All four men helped tie the inept sentries to tree trunks and then began the process of unloading the gold bullion from the vehicle. "Where the hell is Dick with those mules?" one of the robbers asked his cohorts in a panicked voice. "Don't know," replied another. "We'll unload as much as we can, send this buggy on its way, and bury the loot."

The outlaws worked feverishly to remove the riches from the stage and place it into the packs hanging off their horses. When the weight of the gold was nearly overwhelming in the saddles on the overly burdened animals, the bandits remounted and took off.

Horse-drawn wagons filled with supplies and strongboxes were prime targets for highwaymen like Rattlesnake Dick. *Courtesy of Searls Historical Library.*

In the nearby town of Auburn, Dick Barter, better known by most at the time as Rattlesnake Dick, stared anxiously out the narrow window of his jail cell. The bandit in the room with him dragged his scarred knuckles nervously back and forth over the bars. "Think they'll use the jackasses already pulling the shipment to get out?" asked Dick's cellmate. "Doubtful," Dick replied. "The mules are branded. The boys would be stopped by the law as soon as they made it to Folsom."

Dick cursed and took a drag off his cigarette. His job in the robbery was to steal four mules to transport the stolen gold. He and one of his men had been arrested in their attempt to acquire the animals and were now awaiting trial.

If successfully executed, the Wells Fargo gold transport would have been the largest amount ever stolen from a stagecoach. Dick had spent six years honing his criminal skills, robbing single riders, stores, and cabins in preparation for the day he could attempt a rich heist. July 15, 1856, started out as a promising day in the life of the notorious law-breaker, but it ended in a bungled holdup and the vigilante pursuit of his gang.

The devilishly handsome Rattlesnake Dick was born in 1833 in Quebec, Canada. His father was a British Army officer and his French-Canadian mother was a homemaker. They named their oldest son Richard and provided him and his younger sister and brother with comfortable surroundings and a quality education.

Their father's sudden death in 1850 prompted the family to seek its fortune in the United States. The siblings had read about the vast opportunities available there, particularly in the West. The plan was to join an Oregon-bound wagon train in Independence, Missouri. Once the Barters arrived and secured a homestead, they would become ranchers.

Dick made the long journey with his brother, sister, brother-in-law, and cousin. While en route, the Barter brothers and their cousin discussed the exciting news of the Gold Rush. After they made sure their sister and her husband were established in the town of Sweet Home, Oregon, they moved on to California.

Rattlesnake Bar in northern California was one of the richest locations in the West. Gold seekers had converged on the area like locusts. When twenty-year-old Dick and his teenage brother and cousin arrived at the mining district on the American River, they went right to work. Sifting through rocks in the icy water in order to find gold nuggets was not an easy task. It proved to be tough, back-breaking labor for young men who had the idea that the glittery rocks were simply lying around ready to be scooped into a bucket. Within twenty-four hours of arriving at Rattlesnake Bar, Dick's brother and cousin decided to return to Oregon. However, Dick was determined to stick it out.

Regardless of the grueling, tiresome labor Dick was convinced he could locate a rich claim. He raved about the beauty of the scenic mining camp and boasted that Rattlesnake Bar would prove itself to be the best town in the Placers. His optimistic attitude and eager work ethic earned him the name "Rattlesnake Dick."

Dick's insistent will and natural ability earned him as many enemies as friends. Fellow prospectors felt he was "arrogant, vain, and void of that native sense of honor that distinguishes intuitively between right and wrong." Three years after arriving on the Bar, problems between the competing miners and the overly confident Barter arose.

In 1853 several head of livestock had been stolen from a corral near the camp store. A miner who disliked Dick accused him of the crime and Dick was arrested. He was exonerated in court, but he found himself in a similar circumstance a few short months later. This time he was accused of stealing a prospector's mule. The trial that ensued did not have as positive an outcome as the first. Dick was convicted and sentenced to two years in a state prison.

While Dick was being transferred to the penitentiary, word came that another man had confessed to the crime. Barter was released, but the effects of the allegations were permanent. Residents on the Bar treated him as though he were guilty and he felt pressure to move and start over again in another camp.

In early 1854 Barter moved to Shasta County, 150 miles away from his beloved Rattlesnake Bar. He changed his name to Dick Woods and spent every waking hour panning for gold. For two years he lived a quiet, productive life. He was able to eke out a living as a gold miner, but the big strike eluded him. At least Dick was able to elude his past, until the spring of 1856, that is. A series of petty thieves and bandits began terrorizing the mining camps and once again jealous prospectors accused Dick of being behind the crimes. To further complicate matters a resident from Rattlesnake Bar who had been passing through the area recognized Barter and informed residents there of his real name.

Dick was frustrated that his true identity had been made known and that he had to deny yet another charge. "I can stand it no longer," he shouted to the miners around him. "Hereafter my hand is against everyone and I suppose everyone's is against me."

Distraught by the barrage of slanderous accusations, Dick decided he would become the outlaw he was rumored to be. He began his illegal career by holding up a lone traveler riding through the countryside. He told his victim to tell authorities that he had been robbed by "Rattlesnake Dick, the Pirate of the Placers."

Dick's exploits as a solitary highwayman extended over three California counties and included the theft of cattle and horses as well as miner's sluice boxes. (A sluice box is a tool used by prospectors.) Rattlesnake Dick was not content to work alone and in the summer of 1856, he organized a gang of like-minded criminals to help execute even bigger robberies. The men he assembled were ex-convicts and together they robbed stores, homes, and isolated saloons.

The self-proclaimed Pirate of the Placers and his collection of outlaws rendezvoused at an inn near Folsom called the Mountaineer House. It was at this location that Dick laid out plans to rob a Wells Fargo gold shipment. He believed the ambitious job would not only make him rich, but it would also make him the most feared bandit in northern California. His plans unraveled quickly once he was caught stealing the pack mules to be used to carry the gold away.

Rattlesnake Dick's gang panicked at the scene of the holdup when he didn't arrive to help them. They didn't get far with the heavy bags of gold before they realized they couldn't outrun the law hauling the weight of the bullion. They decided to bury half the gold in the hills and return for it at a later date.

The outlaws headed for the spot where they were to meet after the holdup and waited for Dick to arrive. After three anxious days Dick had still not shown. A few of the bandits demanded they be given their share of the money so they could ride on. The majority of the men argued against dividing the gold and insisted on waiting for Dick. The argument became heated and one of the outlaws was shot trying to make off with his cut.

Four of Barter's remaining men decided to return to Auburn to find out what had become of their leader. A posse attempted to apprehend the outlaws on the outskirts of the mining town. One of the bandits was killed in an exchange of gunfire with the law, two were injured, and one was unharmed. All were arrested and escorted to Folsom to stand trial. One of the men was persuaded to lead the law to the area where the gang had buried half of the stolen gold, but he was unable to find the exact location. After several days of searching for the riches, the authorities decided the treasure was lost.

Dick and the fellow gang members who had gotten caught stealing mules escaped from the Auburn jail and fled to San Francisco. He managed to pull together another band of outlaws and they began robbing stages that were traveling between mining camps along the American River.

Placer and Nevada County sheriffs and deputies tracked Dick down and threw him in prison. Every time the bandit was apprehended he would escape. According to early historians, "No jail could hold Barter."

In June 1859, territory officials had had enough of Dick's illegal activities and hired noted lawman John C. Boggs to find the desperado and bring him in dead or alive. Boggs was relentless in his pursuit and paid informers to alert law enforcement if they saw the gangster. On July 11, 1859, a tax collector sent word to the sheriff that Dick had been spotted in the vicinity. Boggs and four of his deputies saddled their horses and rode after the bandits. The lawmen caught up with the robber and his gang a mile outside of Auburn. One of the deputies called out to Rattlesnake Dick, "I'm looking for you!" Dick turned toward the man and shouted back, "Who are you and what do you want?" At that moment Dick drew a weapon from his holster and fired.

After a barrage of shots was exchanged, two of Sheriff Boggs's deputies were injured. As the outlaws fled, the lawmen fired shots at them. One of the bullets hit Rattlesnake Dick in the chest. He almost toppled out of his saddle, but at the last minute straightened up and spurred his horse down the road and out of sight. With only two deputies to accompany him, Boggs decided not to follow Dick any farther. He chose instead to return to Auburn for help.

Several posses were dispatched to scour the countryside for Barter. One posse member spoke with a man who had seen two riders hurrying past his home and reported that one of the riders was reeling in his saddle and the other was supporting him. The following morning Sheriff Boggs received news that Dick's body had been found by a stage driver two miles outside of Auburn.

An affectionate letter from Dick's sister, pleading with him to reform, was found in one of the outlaw's coat pockets. It was dated March 14, 1859, and read, "I ask that you, my beloved brother, the guide of my infant joys, the long lost friend of my childhood, will allow a renewed correspondence to open between you and your good old home."

Rattlesnake Dick's lifeless body was taken to town and laid on the sidewalk in front of the Masonic Hall for a curious crowd to view. He was buried later at the Auburn Cemetery. He was twenty-six years old. The gold his gang stole from the Wells Fargo stage in the summer of 1856 and later buried has never been found.

John and George Sontag and Chris Evans

At War with the Southern Pacific

It was late afternoon on June 12, 1892, when the silhouettes of two men traveling along the wooded hillside of Sampson's Flat in the San Joaquin Valley, California, came into view. A nine-member posse tucked out of sight around the small cabin watched carefully as the duo's long shadows inched toward them. An eager deputy squinted into the low-hanging sun and grinned. "They're the men we've been looking for," he said in a low, confident voice. He raised his Winchester rifle to his shoulder and fired at the pair. Outlaw John Sontag, a modestly built man in his early thirties, who walked with a limp and sported a long, droopy mustache, was jerked backward by a bullet that caught him in the right shoulder.

Fellow bandit Chris Evans, a mountain of a man with dark, unruly hair and a massive, unkempt beard, pulled his six-shooter from his holster and returned fire. Bullets rushed passed his frame, hitting the trees around him. Undeterred by the lethal barrage, Evans calmly reloaded his weapon and continued firing at the posse. One of his shots shattered a cabin window; a second and third bullet plunged into the doorframe. Several others hit their marks and lawmen lay strewn about.

It was nightfall before the battle ended. When the smoke from the gunfire that had been exchanged cleared, four members of the posse were dead, Sontag was seriously injured and resting against a straw-and-manure pile, and Evans had escaped. A couple of deputies searched the area and found blood on a trail leading away from the scene. They knew Evans had been hurt and hoped he wouldn't get far.

The weary lawmen returned to the nearest town with Sontag in tow and immediately formed another posse. The search for the notorious train robbers had lasted nine months and determined sheriffs and deputies were not about to abandon the chase.

Since their first train robbery in January 1889, John Sontag, his brother George, and their friend Chris Evans had stolen $15,000 from the Southern Pacific Railroad. The clash in Fresno County hadn't been the only time the law had shot it out with Evans and the Sontags. The men had been cornered before and managed to get away. Railroad executives were frustrated and wanted the outlaws brought in dead or alive.

The war between the Southern Pacific Railroad, the Sontags, and Evans began in the late 1800s. John, the oldest of two sons, was born to Maria and Jacob Contant on May 27, 1861, in Mankato, Minnesota, and was employed as a brakeman for the line in 1887. While on the job in Fresno, the twenty-six-year-old was seriously injured when he accidentally became stuck between two cars being pushed together by the engine. During his convalescence the railroad let him go. Sontag was furious and because of the severity of his injury was unable to find employment quickly.

John's animosity and resentment toward the executives at Southern Pacific was shared by many in the area. When the line had been initially laid out in 1880, the railroad owners swindled settlers along the route out of their property. Southern Pacific land appraisers and their henchmen evicted homesteaders living on railroad property if they refused to pay an adjusted price to stay.

In September of 1880, a group of twenty bitter settlers gathered in the town of Hanford to protest the unfair business dealings of Southern Pacific. A gunfight between railroad workers and the homesteaders erupted and five men were killed.

Sentiment against the Southern Pacific Railroad ran high after the

The posse that captured the Sontags and Chris Evans stands over the body of the mortally wounded John Sontag. *Courtesy of Searls Historical Library.*

incident and any man who opposed the organization was regarded as a patriot. John Sontag would eventually use that attitude to his advantage.

Chris Evans, a farmer in the vicinity, who had once studied to be a priest, knew of Sontag's misfortune and offered him a job at his livery stable and ranch. Evans was not a fan of the Southern Pacific Railroad either. He felt their excessive freight rates were highway robbery. Fueled by their hatred for the railroad, the two men decided to exact their revenge.

The first train robbery Sontag and Evans orchestrated in Goshen, California, on January 21, 1889, enabled the pair to make off with $600 from the line's express car. On February 21, 1889, the men robbed another Southern Pacific train outside of Pixley. This time the duo stole $5,000. If residents in the town of Visalia, where Sontag and Evans based their operations, suspected the two were involved in the crimes, they never came forward. Many of the people in the area were pleased that the railroad was suffering. As the outlaws had arrived on the other side of the heists undetected, Sontag and Evans decided to wait awhile before orchestrating their next job.

Evans returned to his farm and John returned to Minnesota to visit his brother, George. Born on April 10, 1864, George had had his own run-ins with the law. While still living at home with his mother and stepfather (Matthias Sontag, from whom he and John took their family name), he was caught stealing money from the store where he was working. At seventeen he was sentenced to six years in the state penitentiary. He escaped after only serving one year, but he returned later to finish his time.

During John's visit with George, John shared with his brother the news of the railroad holdups and invited George to join him on the next job. George declined, but John hoped he'd change his mind. John returned to Visalia and he and Evans reunited outside of the town of Ceres. Their planned robbery was thwarted by a Southern Pacific Railroad detective. Shaken by the encounter with the law, the men again went their separate ways.

By the time John returned to his home town in the upper Midwest, George had reconsidered his offer to partner with him. The brothers began making plans to hold up a train running between two popular Minnesota River towns. On November 5, 1891, the Sontags stole $9,800 from the Southern Pacific Railroad express car. After the holdup they raced back to California.

George and John fled to Evans's place to hide out. While they were there, the three men decided to steal the railroad's payroll, being shipped on a passenger train out of Alila.

The outlaws traveled part of the way to the scene of the impending crime on horseback. A mile or two from the location of the theft, the men then secured their horses to a tree, walked back to the depot, snuck aboard the train, and hid out in a baggage car. When the time was right, they covered their faces with masks, overtook the engineer, and ordered him to stop the engine. Then they blew open the safe in the express car with dynamite.

Frustrated with their own attempts to apprehend the criminals, the executives at the Southern Pacific Railroad solicited help from the Pinkerton Detective Agency. A full-scale investigation to learn the identity of the thieves was launched.

Confident they had devised a foolproof way of robbing trains, the Sontags and Chris Evans made arrangements for another holdup. On August 1, 1892, the outlaws robbed a train leaving Collis Station in Fresno. To avoid detection the men went their separate ways after the theft.

John and Chris hurried to the rendezvous point in Visalia; George abandoned his horse outside of Fresno and boarded the very train he and his cohorts had robbed a short time before. The passengers were talking excitedly among themselves about the crime. George interjected himself into the conversation and encouraged the travelers to recount the adventure down to the smallest detail.

Detectives on the scene after the robbery, who were told about the way George was behaving, were immediately suspicious. Passengers informed the authorities that the curious man was George Sontag, a resident of the area. Sontag was ordered to the sheriff's office for questioning. George withstood the interrogation for a few hours before admitting his guilt. In order to avoid prosecution and being sent to the gallows, he named his brother and Evans as his accomplices.

In anticipation that both bandits would be hiding out at Evans's farm, the Pinkertons secretly hurried to its location. The outlaws were there and as the posse closed in, Sontag and Evans shot their way out. John Sontag and Evans gunned down three detectives before escaping. The public was outraged.

The headline across the front page of the September 14, 1892, edition of the *San Francisco Examiner* read, "A Wanton Butchery, Evans and Sontag Attack a Pursuing Posse." The newspaper owner, William Randolph Hearst, encouraged the men hunting the pair to "enter upon the chase with the intention of killing the blood thirsty desperadoes."

More than a year was spent searching for the outlaws, who were rumored to be hiding in the San Joaquin Valley. During that time George

Sontag was tried and sentenced to life in prison. Settlers who continued to harbor ill feelings toward the unfair land dealings of the Southern Pacific Railroad helped keep the Pinkertons off John Sontag's and Chris Evans's trail. The desperadoes sent word to their pursuers that they had declared open war on them and that they would shoot and kill any detectives they encountered. A $10,000 reward was offered for the pair and more than one thousand men were involved in the various posses to bring them to justice.

The bandits lost their battle with the law in the summer of 1892. Apache scouts hired by Wells Fargo led authorities to a cabin several miles outside of Visalia. When the arresting officers approached the building the desperadoes inside opened fire. The Indian trailers returned the shots hitting their targets, but not killing them. A fatally wounded John Sontag was taken into custody on the spot and he died three weeks after his arrest.

Evans was captured forty-eight hours later a few yards from the scene of the shootout. He was seriously injured, but he made a full recovery and was tried on November 28, 1892. He was found guilty of murder and robbery and sentenced to life in prison. A month after being interned at Folsom Prison, Evans escaped and made his way back to his ranch in Visalia. A posse tracked the convicted outlaw down again on February 19, 1894, and he was returned to Folsom Prison.

After serving fifteen years behind bars, George Sontag was pardoned. He moved to San Francisco and lived out the remainder of his days working part time at a gambling resort. In 1909 the autobiography he coauthored with Opie Warner, entitled *A Pardoned Lifer,* was published. Sontag then embarked on a speaking tour across the United States, lecturing on life as an outlaw.

Chris Evans also became an author. His book, *Eurasia,* was published in 1910. In 1911 he too was pardoned. He was banned from living in California, however, and relocated to Oregon. Evans died in 1917. George Sontag was pardoned in 1908, and the last documented reference to George appeared in a Minnesota newspaper in 1929.

Dick Fellows

No Credit to His Profession

Dick Fellows, a thick, stocky man with a curly, black beard, took a long drag off a cigarette and flicked the butt onto the ground. A cold wind swept the smoldering stub over a dense wooded trail leading to the town of Caliente in Kern County. Fellows watched the cigarette for a moment then jerked the reins of the horse standing beside him and pulled the animal closer to block the frigid rush of air. Darkness was closing in and a worried expression froze his face. "Stage should be along any minute," Fellows reassured himself and his restless mount. His plans to rob the Wells Fargo stage carrying $240,000 in gold included the help of just one other man. He was waiting down the road to transport the shipment to their hideout once they pulled off the robbery.

It was December 4, 1875. Fellows whistled a jaunty holiday tune as he imagined all he could do with nearly a quarter of a million dollars.

Somewhere in the near distance he heard the sound of a team of horses and the durable wheels of the coach traveling over the rocky terrain. Still whistling, he tied a handkerchief to the lower half of his face and tried to climb atop the skittish mare. The horse stepped away from Fellows refusing to allow him to sit on her back. The stage was drawing closer and Fellows was becoming frustrated with the animal's stubborn behavior. He finally jerked the horse into submission and jumped aboard.

Fellows's difficulties with the horse continued. The animal had a mind of its own and would not move in the direction its rider wanted. She trotted away from the path the stage would soon be passing. No amount of coaxing or force would persuade the mare to do anything Fellows desired. It wasn't until the gold shipment had raced by and was

Dick Fellows spent years in California prisons for his crimes.
Courtesy of Searls Historical Library.

out of sight that the horse broke into a frantic gallop—in the opposite direction. Fellows pulled back on the reins and the animal began to buck.

Like a determined rodeo cowboy, the would-be outlaw held on to the saddle rejecting the fierce attempts to throw him. The horse continued her kicking and rearing and eventually flung Fellows off the backend. He landed hard on his head and was knocked unconscious. The mare quickly trotted away from the scene as Fellows lay motionless in the middle of the trail. His partner on the job rode away from the scene the minute Fellows lost control of the horse.

When Fellows came to he was dazed, but not disillusioned. He brushed himself off, walked back to the nearest town, rented another horse, and set out to hold up the same Wells Fargo stage on its return trip. Unfortunately that plan was fraught with just as many obstacles as the first. The northbound stage out of Los Angeles was right on schedule as it traveled along the narrow wagon road that wound between Caliente and Bakersfield. Fellows's horse did not balk as he led him onto the path of the approaching vehicle. The stage driver stopped the carriage when Fellows leveled a gun at him and quickly threw down the strongbox as ordered.

After Fellows sent the stage on its way he realized he'd forgotten to bring the necessary tools to open the box. He was forced to drag the safe off the trail and consider alternate ways to break into the metal package. While Fellows was trying to force the lock open, the sun descended on the horizon. There was no moon that night and he had a hard time seeing well enough to locate the right rock to help him get into the safe.

The horse that had been shuffling alongside Fellows as he worked suddenly became spooked by the persistent banging on the box and took off without him. The unfortunate bandit ran after the animal, but when he became concerned that he would lose track of the strongbox, he turned back.

Undeterred by the horse's behavior, Fellows hoisted the safe on his shoulders and started walking. He knew a posse would soon be on his trail and he needed to find a place to hide out. He fumbled along in the dark for some time before he happened onto an abandoned railroad camp. Unbeknownst to Fellows, an open eighteen-foot tunnel stood in the way of him and a rundown shack where he could take cover. The long fall down broke his leg and ankle.

The injured Fellows struggled to pull himself and the safe out of the tunnel. Once he was out he placed the strongbox on the ground in front of him and began pushing it. He finally reached the tent of a Chinese railroad worker living near the Tehachapi Creek. Before tending to his bruises and breaks, Fellows used the man's ax to break the lock on the box. Inside was $1,800. He pocketed the money, fashioned a pair of crutches out of tree branches, and hobbled to a nearby farm.

Wells Fargo detective Jim Hume, and the relentless posse with him, searched Kern County for twenty-six hours before catching up with the slow-moving Fellows. Hume arrested Fellows and the luckless outlaw was incarcerated at the nearest jail in Bakersfield.

Dick Fellows was born George Brittain Lytle in Clay County, Kentucky, in 1846. He left home at the age of twenty-five and came west to go into the hog-farming business with a friend. When the business went bankrupt, the discouraged Fellows decided to become an outlaw. He changed his name after holding up his first stage in November of 1869, stealing $300. He orchestrated his second holdup a week later by disguising tree branches as men in order to trick drivers into thinking there was more than one person in on the robbery. Within a month of the crimes, he was arrested. He pled guilty to both robberies and was ordered to serve ten years at San Quentin.

While on the inside he made good use of his time. He studied religion and got a job working as the facility's librarian. He was an inspiration to other inmates, leading Bible studies and helping them to turn their lives around through education. One of the prisoners wrote in his journal that Fellows had "a vigor and eloquence that struck tremors in the souls of the minions of Satan." California governor Newton Booth was so impressed with Fellows's rehabilitation efforts that he granted him a full pardon on April 4, 1874.

Eighteen months after his release from prison, he reverted to his old ways. He was residing in Caliente and making every effort to live an honorable life when he heard a rumor about a large gold shipment being transported to Los Angeles. After noticing four guards at the town depot board a Wells Fargo stage, he determined the rumor was true and started plotting to hold up the carriage. He robbed it on December 4, 1875.

The December 7, 1875, edition of the *Kern County Weekly Courier* reported on the unsuccessful holdup and renamed Fellows "Lame Dick." "He gave himself up with no trouble," the article read. "He did not appear to know that he was arrested for stealing a horse (the frightened animal that ran off never to return), but took it for granted that it was for robbing the stage."

At his hearing on June 8, 1876, Fellows was sentenced to eight years at his old stomping grounds, San Quentin. He was waiting to be transported to the prison when he escaped. The tenacious outlaw pried away the planks on the cell floor and snuck out through a small tunnel.

He made his way to the banks of the Kern River and hid in the brush and trees along the water's edge. Fellows waited two days before venturing out of his hiding place and limping to a nearby farmhouse. From there he stole a plow horse and tried to make a fast getaway out of the area.

Once again the horse he chose had other plans. The animal fought the outlaw while Fellows was trying to get on his back, and eventually it broke free. Fellows watched in disbelief as the horse disappeared over a hill in the direction of the farm they had just come from. While contemplating his next course of action, an angry posse converged on the scene. He was immediately bound and gagged and escorted to prison.

The crowd that surrounded the criminal as he was being led into the gates of San Quentin numbered more than seven hundred people. Many of those curious onlookers claimed to have had a hand in Fellows's capture. In a letter to Detective Hume, Fellows strongly criticized the mob for taking credit for his incarceration. "They are a crowd of nincom-poops," Fellows wrote. "They even had the bad taste to divert from their legitimate calling of sheepherders in order to add to the distress of an unfortunate fellow-being who was only endeavoring to flee the country.

"As they crowded around, each discussing his relative importance in effecting my capture, I could not help thinking (save the profane com-parison) that unless shepherds had woefully degenerated since Oriental times, the infant Jesus himself would have met short shrift at their hands, if Herod had had the foresight to offer a suitable reward."

Dick Fellows behaved admirably behind bars just as he had done during his previous incarceration. He was again put in charge of the library and gave every indication that he had officially turned his life around . . . again. When he was released in May of 1881, he promised prison officials that he would "try to live honestly within the pale of society." Fellows hoped to find work as a teacher. During his stay in jail, he learned to speak and write fluent Spanish and sought employment as a professor of the language. Using the alias G. Brett Lytle, he placed an advertisement looking for students in the *Santa Cruz Daily Echo*. No one responded.

In July of 1881, he abandoned his search for legitimate work and returned to robbing stages. For six months he "terrorized" the trails from San Francisco to San Luis Obispo. The woefully obstinate outlaw held up five stages during that time and stole a total of $10. Wells Fargo agents had sent out several decoy gold shipments in order to fool the crook. Their efforts proved effective.

Deputies in a posse out of Santa Cruz finally tracked Fellows to a cabin in Los Gatos. The sentence that followed his capture and trial in 1882 was life in prison. Fellows broke out of his holding cell one more time and got away. He found a horse tied to a hitching post two blocks from the jail, hopped on the animal's back, and urged the roan into a gallop.

A few moments into the ride the horse started bucking and kicking uncontrollably. Fellows hung on to the boney neck of the steed, but it could not stop the inevitable. The horse threw him to the ground and the sheriff and deputies rushed in and cuffed the outlaw. During the trip back to jail, Fellows learned that the horse had been suffering from the effects of eating a hallucinogenic plant.

Before being granted another pardon in 1908, Fellows was made a teacher in the Department of Moral Instruction at Folsom Prison. He also worked as a chaplain's assistant and tutored inmates. Detective Jim Hume and Wells Fargo president John J. Valentine agreed that Fellows had redeemed himself and believed the former bandit should be returned to decent society.

What became of Fellows after his release remains a mystery. Historians speculate that he returned to Kentucky and lived out the rest of his days teaching school. No death certificate exists for the luckless outlaw.

Joaquin Murieta
The Bandito Who Lost His Head

In August 1853, a parade of stone-faced pioneers filtered into the lobby of a crowded, brick courthouse in Marysville, California. They talked among themselves in low, hushed tones as the line they waited in slowly advanced toward a table at the front of the corridor. Two large glass jars sat in the center of the table. Inside one of the containers was a human hand; in the other, a human head. The severed hand and head were bloated and floating eerily in a clear liquid. The morbidly curious onlookers gaped in astonishment at the sight, elbowing one another and pointing.

A slim, slip of a girl with long, dark hair shook with great sobs as she followed along behind the others. She blinked away the tears while forcing herself to look upon the disembodied face in the jar. For several minutes she stood frozen in one spot. The people behind her urged her on, but she wouldn't move.

Escorted by a deputy, Sacramento County judge O. P. Stridger, a thick, short-bodied man, strode over to the grieving woman. On their way they walked past a giant sandwich board sign that read, EXHIBITION: ONE DAY ONLY! THE HEAD OF THE BANDIT JOAQUIN AND THE HAND OF BANDIT THREE-FINGERED JACK.

"Young lady," Judge Stridger softly spoke, "Are you all right?" The distressed woman wiped her eyes with the shawl covering her shoulders and nodded. A slight smile of relief gradually spread over her tormented face. "That's not my brother," she sighed. "What?" the judge asked incredulously. He exchanged a troubled look with the deputy next to them. "Joaquin Murieta was your brother?" he further inquired. "Si," she answered. "But that's not him." Her eyes looked from the judge to the deputy and back at the head in the jar. "Who is it?" the deputy quickly inquired. "It is Joaquin Gonzales," she told them.

The perplexed men watched the woman step out of the line and make her way through the eager viewers who continued to press in on the exhibit. "Captain Love swears this is the bandit Murieta," the deputy reminded Judge Stridger in a low voice. The judge stood thinking for a moment and then reached into his pocket, removed a cigar as fat as a baby's leg, and lit it. "Let's hope Captain Love is right," he said taking a long puff off his stogie.

The judge glanced up in the direction of the door just as the woman was exiting the building. A blast of sunlight erased his view of her departure. For a split second he considered following after her and questioning her further about her brother. The well-attended spectacle before him made him change his mind. He took another drag from his cigar and turned his attention back to the ill-fated deceased.

Joaquin Murieta was one of many bandits who drifted from mining camp to mining camp in the early 1850s. The seventy-five men who made up his gang helped him steal horses, hold up stages, raid farmhouses, and rob prospectors. They slit the throats of many of their victims and left settlements fearful of their violent return. Had it not been for the creative pen of journalist John Rollin Ridge, this man Murieta, known as the chief of bandits, would simply have been remembered as another ruthless Old West outlaw.

Ridge's fictionalized version of Joaquin Murieta transformed him into a folk hero. His book, entitled *The Life and Adventures of Joaquin Murieta,* was first published in 1854. Since that time, Murieta's actual wrongdoings and the motivation behind his criminal activity have been overshadowed by Ridge's romantic version of his dastardly deeds.

Most historians agree that Joaquin was born in Sonora, Mexico, in 1832, and that his surname was Carrillo. An 1855 edition of the *San Francisco Call* boasts that he grew to be a man of "refined appearance, with a high forehead crowned with a blanket of hair and endowed with gracious manners." His parents sent him to school in Mexico City. When his education was complete, Joaquin took a job in the country's president's stables and worked as a groomsman. At seventeen he returned home and married a girl from his village named Carmen Rosita Feliz and the two decided to build a life for themselves in California. Murieta had heard the cry of "gold" echoing from the riverbanks of the American River in the northern portion of the state and believed that that was where his future lay.

The prospectors who had already staked out sizeable claims for themselves resented one more miner vying for the gold in the area. Many white miners who wanted to see the native people in the region driven out particularly resented Mexicans and Indians panning or digging alongside them.

The unfriendly reception Joaquin and his bride, Carmen, experienced when they arrived in Stanislaus County had a strong impact. Time and time again the young couple were driven from the piece of earth where they decided to search for gold. When Murieta resisted his claim being jumped, it usually resulted in a serious beating. Bitter and angry, he abandoned his gold-mining venture and brooded over his unfortunate circumstances. He explained to his wife that his job opportunities were limited and that it seemed he was being forced to become a bandit. Deciding she would be better off without him, he left Carmen behind and headed off to the town of Murphy.

Before committing entirely to the lifestyle of an outlaw, he tried his luck at gambling. After losing all he had in a game of monte, he threw himself into the murky depths of crime. There were several disenfranchised men in the same situation as Murieta, Mexican natives and desperadoes of other nationalities deemed outcasts. Equipped with a strong personality and leadership ability, Murieta was able to unite these renegades.

In November 1851, Murieta and his gang held up a number of stages traveling between the mining camps of Calaveras and Tuolumne Counties. They also stole more than three hundred head of horses and

Joaquin Murieta was the most feared and most wanted outlaw in California.

Courtesy of Searls Historical Library.

drove them to Mexico to be sold. They left several dead bodies in the wake of each crime. Victims weren't just murdered, they were flogged, beaten, and had their throats cut. Oftentimes the outlaws would throw a lariat around the neck of a victim and drag the person around until the body was unrecognizable. Among the savage men who rode with the man many now referred to as Bloody Joaquin Murieta were Three-Fingered Jack, Reyes Feliz, and Joaquin Valenzuela. Valenzuela was one of three men named Joaquin who kept company with Murieta. Three-Fingered Jack is credited with killing six Chinese miners found tied together by their queues (long braids of hair that reached down their backs), with their heads nearly severed from their torsos.

In the winter of 1851, Murieta orchestrated a spree of robberies and raids on campsites that resulted in twenty-three murders in the area around Chico, California. Settlers were outraged by the brutal attacks and fearful for their lives. Posses and vigilante committees were formed, but Murieta was able to elude his pursuers by taking unknown routes and brush-covered pathways. He would split his men into small groups and travel under cover of darkness. He had contacts in various towns and mining camps, unsavory characters who would benefit monetarily if they let the bandit chief know the location of approaching law enforcement officers.

By the spring of 1853, Murieta's reign of terror had extended into the southern half of California. He invaded homesteads, stealing cattle and personal belongings; held up supply wagons making their way from one outpost to the next; and robbed some of the isolated saloons that dotted the territory.

Before robbing saloon-keepers of their nightly earnings, he would engage the gamblers on hand in a game of poker. On one particular occasion Murieta sat opposite a drunken dealer who was shuffling a deck and eyeing the menacing-looking desperado. With a hint of recognition in his voice the gambler exclaimed, "I'd give $1,000 for a chance at that greaser Murieta." Murieta sneered and removed a knife from his pocket.

He leaned over the man and placed the tip of the blade against his temple. "You damned gringo," he whispered in his ear. "I am Murieta." A panicked look twisted the inebriated man's face. He gently pushed himself away from the table and slowly backed out of the saloon.

Settlers and landowners tired of being held hostage by the lawless element that drifted unchallenged from county to county. California governor John Bigler was compelled to take serious action and on May 11, 1853, he signed a legislative act creating the California State Rangers, whose reason for existence was to bring in the Murieta gang, known as the "Five Joaquins." The act specifically targeted the handful of men with that name who were either leaders or members of the gang.

Reward money was appropriated to apprehend the fugitives and wanted posters were circulated. The price on Joaquin Murieta's head was $5,000. The bandit noticed his wanted poster while passing through Stockton. He studied the petition, carefully reading the words aloud to himself: "$5,000 to the one who delivers Joaquin Murieta. Dead or Alive." In a cool, unflinching manner, the bandit removed a pencil from his pocket and scribbled a message on the bottom of the poster. Townspeople dared to inspect the poster only after Murieta and his gang had ridden off. The defiant outlaw had written, "I will give $10,000. Joaquin."

The mounted rangers were empowered to "arrest, drive out of the country, or exterminate the numerous gangs which continually placed in danger the life and property of all citizens." Captain Harry Love, a Texas army scout and the deputy sheriff of Los Angeles, was hired to lead the manhunt.

The twenty members of Love's California Rangers enlisted for a ninety-day period, were paid $150 a month, and promised $1,000 reward for apprehending the criminals. The majority of the rangers had shady pasts. They were murderers and thieves hoping to make a name for themselves in law enforcement. Love had a reputation as a cowardly braggart and believed capturing any of the Joaquins would change the public's perception of him.

Murieta was aware of Love and his rangers and had decided to return to Sonora with the thousands of dollars in cash he had illegally acquired, as well as the horses he had stolen. His plan was to stay ahead of the posse that was after him while organizing a series of raids on river schooners near Stockton before heading back to Mexico.

Love led a determined chase. Time and again he and his men were on the verge of overtaking Murieta when their efforts were thwarted by Mexican natives fearful of what Murieta might do to them if they did not protect the bandit. Murieta employed the same successful escape tactics he had always used. He divided his large band of thieves into smaller groups and had them go separate ways. Under these conditions tracking the bandit down was an arduous task.

In July 1853, two months after Love's search began, the captain took seven of his men into the San Joaquin Valley to investigate a column of smoke they'd seen in the distance. According to Captain Love's account, they followed the smoke to a group of men seated around a campfire. Love asked the men where they were going.

"One of the bandits," Love later recounted, "replied that they were traveling to Los Angeles. At this juncture another member of the group addressed me, and insolently told me that if I had any further inquiries to make to address them to him, as he was the leader of the party. I replied that I was an American officer, and as such spoke when, how and to whom I pleased. The man made a quick move as if to reach for his gun, when I warned that a single move would provide him with a quick exit from this world."

The leader of the gang was identified by one of the California Rangers as Joaquin Murieta. Knowing they had been found out, Murieta and his men quickly scattered and rushed to their waiting horses. Joaquin made it to his horse, but the animal was shot out from under him. The bandit toppled over his mount and landed hard onto the ground. The frantic and dazed outlaw got to his feet and started to run away. His body was hit with a volley of bullets. He fell again and this time he was dead. Joaquin's followers were also killed. Three-Fingered Jack was chased for five miles before Love shot him in the head.

Captain Love anticipated that his dubious past might prompt skeptics to question whether the notorious outlaw Murieta was indeed dead. To prove the shooting took place, Love ordered Joaquin's head and Three-Fingered Jack's hand to be cut off and preserved in alcohol-filled jars. He returned to the state capital with his prize in tow. Love was immediately presented with a $1,000 reward, plus a bonus of $5,000. The bandits' remains were put on display at county jails and saloons. Visitors came from miles around to view the human trophies.

Not everyone agreed that the man Love killed was Murieta. The editor of the *San Francisco Alta* investigated the claim and determined that the ambitious captain had gunned down someone other than the outlaw in question.

"It affords amusement to our citizens to read the various accounts of the capture and decapitation of 'the notorious Joaquin Murieta.' The humbug is so transparent that it is surprising any sensible person can be imposed upon by the statements of the affairs which have appeared in the prints.

"A few weeks ago a party of native Americans and Sonorians started for Tulara Valley for the expressed and avowed purpose of running mustangs. Three of the party have returned and report that they were attacked by a party of Americans and the balance of their party, four in number, had been killed; that Joaquin Valenzuela, one of them, was killed as he was endeavoring to escape and that his head was cut off and taken as a trophy.

"It is too well known that Joaquin Murieta was not in the party nor was he the person killed by Captain Harry Love's party at the Panache Pass. The head recently exhibited in Stockton bears no resemblance to that individual, and this is positively asserted by those who have seen the real Murieta and the spurious head."

The *Alta* editor's article, which appeared on August 19, 1853, raised doubts among many readers about whether the remains of the man the Rangers brought in and displayed were those of Murieta. The controversy did not stop people from attending public viewings of the deceased remains, however. Murieta's sister, a resident of Marysville, openly objected to the barbaric display. She went to her grave insisting her brother had escaped to Mexico and lived out his days with his second wife and their children. Her claim was supported by a few who had seen Murieta years after his supposed death.

Captain Harry Love never deviated from his assertion that he had killed Joaquin Murieta. Love died on June 29, 1868, from a wound received in a gunfight with one of his employees.

Joaquin's head toured California for more than thirty years before being put on permanent display at Dr. Jordan's Museum of Horrors in San Francisco. The exhibit was destroyed in the great earthquake of 1906.

The life of Joaquin Murieta was a violent affair, accentuated by thievery, killings, and narrow escapes. A handful of sympathetic newspaper men in the mid-1850s suggested he was propelled by vengeance and the need to regain the dignity he felt the "blue-eyed gringos" stole from him.

Reporter, magazine writer, and poet John Rollin Ridge agreed. Ridge's own past had been mired by murders and prejudice and he identified with the notion that Murieta was misunderstood and desperate for acceptance.

Ridge, a Cherokee Indian from Georgia, was struggling to find a way to make ends meet when he decided to write about the outlaw. Using the basic facts of Murieta's life, he created an intriguing story, built on the traditional Robin Hood tale. Ridge's main character was a man of "generous and noble nature, built like a tiger and unafraid to challenge mistreatment from white men."

Historians believe Ridge saw himself in the legend he'd created. The hopeful author expected to earn a great deal of money from the book, but his publisher was less than honest and he never made a dime. "After selling 7,000 copies," Ridge wrote in a letter to his cousin in Oklahoma, "he put the money in his own pockets; fled, and left me and a hundred others to whistle for our money."

Since the release of Ridge's book in 1854, numerous other authors have written about Joaquin Murieta. Many books and magazine articles merely reworked Ridge's original material, plagiarizing some of the dialogue. In 1938 Hollywood made a movie based on Ridge's book, aptly titled, *Joaquin Murieta*.

John Rollin Ridge died in 1867 at the age of forty. He is remembered as the Old West's first desperado image maker to turn legend into history. More than 150 years after his death, Joaquin Murieta—whatever his fate—is still recognized as one of California's most notorious outlaws.

Bibliography

Birmingham, Stephen. *California Rich*. New York: Simon & Schuster, 1980.

Borthwick, John D. *The Gold Hunters*. Wales: MacMillan Publishing, 1917.

Brock, M. J. and W. B. Lardner. *History of Placer & Nevada Counties*. Los Angeles: Historic Record Company, 1924.

Carson, James H. *Recollections of California Mines*. Oakland, Cal.: Biobooks, 1950.

Haslam, Gerald W. *Coming of Age in California*. Walnut Creek, Cal.: Devil Mountain Books, 2000.

Horan, James D. *The Authentic Wild West*. New York: Crown Publishers, 1977.

Houston, James. *Californians: Searching for the Golden State*. New York: Knopf Publishing, 1992.

Jackson, Joseph H. *Bad Company*. New York: Harcourt, Brace, 1946.

Jones, Thomas. *You Bet: How the California Miners Did It*. New York: New Publishing Company, 1936.

Loya, Joe. *The Man Who Outgrew His Prison Cell*. New York: Rayo Publishing, 2004.

Nash, Jay R. *Encyclopedia of Western Lawmen & Outlaws*. New York: Paragon House, 1989.

National Police Gazette, XL, no. 239 (April 22, 1882).

Oppel, Frank. *Tales of California*. San Francisco: Castle Books, 1989.

Real West Magazine, VIII, no. 42 (July 1965).

Real West Magazine, VIII, no. 43 (September 1965).

Sann, Paul and James Horan. *Pictorial History of the Wild West*. New York: Bonanza Books, 1965.

Secrest, William B. *Perilous Trails, Dangerous Men: Early California Stagecoach Robbers and Their Desperate Careers*. Clovis, Cal.: Word Dancer Press, 2002.

Thurston, Clarke. *California Fault*. New York: Ballantine Books, 1996.

Tom Bell

MacDonald, Franklin. *Eight Weeks to Sundown*. San Francisco: Pacific Bell, 1984.

Tiburcio Vasquez

Chronicles of the Old West, 4, no. 6 (May 2004).

Henshall, John A. "Tales of the Early California Bandits." *Overland Monthly* (1909).

Henry Plummer

Allen, Frederick. *A Decent Orderly Lynching*. Norman: University of Oklahoma Press, 2004.

Mather, R. E. and R. E. Boswell, *Hanging the Sheriff.* Provo: University of Utah Press, 1987.

Nevada County Historical Society Bulletin, 49, no. 4 (October 1995).

Charles Earl "Black Bart" Boles

Collins, William. *Black Bart: The True Story of the West's Most Famous Stagecoach Robber.* Mendocino, Cal.: Pacific Transcripts, 1992.

Dajania, Laika. *Black Bart: Elusive Highwaymen.* Manhattan, Kans.: Sunflower University Press, 1996.

Hoeper, George. *Black Bart: Boulevardier Bandit.* Fresno, Cal.: Word Dancer Press, 1995.

Hume, J. B. *Wells, Fargo & Co.* San Francisco: Wells, Fargo Books, 1888.

Jesús Tejada

San Francisco Morning Call, January 7, 1888.

Juan Flores

Cox, Bill. "Back-Country Bad Man." *High Country Magazine* (June 1968).

"Rattlesnake Dick" Barter

McLeod, Norman. "Rattlesnake Dick." *Sierra Heritage Magazine* (August 1972).

John and George Sontag and Chris Evans

Indianapolis Sentinel, June 13, 1893.

Maxwell, Hue. *Evans & Sontag: The Famous Bandits of California.* San Francisco: San Francisco Printing Company, 1981.

San Francisco Examiner, September 14, 1892.

Sontag, John. *A Pardoned Lifer.* San Bernardino, Cal.: The Index Print, 1909.

Joaquin Murieta

Block, Eugene B. *Great Stagecoach Robbers of the West.* New York: Doubleday, 1962.

Henshall, John A. "A Bandit of the Golden Age." *Overland Monthly* (July 1963).

Ridge, John R. *The Life & Adventures of Joaquin Murieta.* Norman: University of Oklahoma Press, 1855.

Index

About the Author

Chris Enss is an award-winning screenwriter who has written for television, short subject films, live performances, and the movies. Enss has done everything from stand-up comedy to working as a stunt person at the Old Tucson Movie Studio. She learned the basics of writing for film and television at the University of Arizona, and she is currently working with *Return of the Jedi* producer Howard Kazanjian on the movie version of *The Cowboy and the Senorita*, their biography of western stars Roy Rogers and Dale Evans.

"Courage is being scared to death—
and saddling up anyway."

—*John Wayne*

Discover all the TwoDot® books
at www.globepequot.com

3 1143 00922 3596

TwoDot® is an imprint of
The Globe Pequot Press